3rd Edition Extra

with business skills lessons and self-assessment

Elementary

MARKET LEADER

Business English Course Book

David Cotton   David Falvey   Simon Kent

with Nina O'Driscoll

FT Publishing
FINANCIAL TIMES

GLOBAL SCALE
of English

Contents

Introduction

What is *Market Leader*, and who is it for?

Market Leader is a multi-level business English course for businesspeople and students of business English. It has been developed in association with the *Financial Times*, one of the leading sources of business information in the world. It consists of 12 units based on topics of great interest to everyone involved in international business.

This third edition of the Elementary level features completely updated content and a significantly enhanced range of authentic resource material, reflecting the latest trends in the business world. If you are in business, the course will greatly improve your ability to communicate in English in a wide range of business situations. If you are a student of business, the course will develop the communication skills you need to succeed in business and will enlarge your knowledge of the business world. Everybody studying this course will become more fluent and confident in using the language of business and should increase their career prospects.

The authors

David Falvey (left) has over 25 years' teaching and managerial experience in the UK, Japan and Hong Kong. He has also worked as a teacher trainer at the British Council in Tokyo, and was Head of the English Language Centre and Principal Lecturer at London Metropolitan University.

David Cotton (centre) has over 45 years' experience teaching and training in EFL, ESP and English for Business, and is the author of numerous business English titles, including *Agenda*, *World of Business*, *International Business Topics* and *Keys to Management*. He is also one of the authors of the best-selling *Business Class*. He was previously a Senior Lecturer at London Metropolitan University.

Simon Kent (right) has over 25 years' teaching experience, including three years as an in-company trainer in Berlin at the time of German reunification. He has spent the majority of his career to date in higher education in the UK where he has taught on and directed programmes of business, general and academic English.

What is in the units?

STARTING UP

You are offered a variety of interesting activities in which you discuss the topic of the unit and exchange ideas about it.

VOCABULARY

You will learn important new words and phrases which you can use when you carry out the tasks in the unit. You can find definitions and examples, and listen to the pronunciation of new vocabulary in the i-Glossary feature on the DVD-ROM. The DVD-ROM also contains practice exercises. A good business dictionary, such as the *Longman Business English Dictionary*, will also help you to increase your business vocabulary.

READING

You will read authentic articles on a variety of topics from the *Financial Times* and other newspapers and books on business. You will develop your reading skills and learn essential business vocabulary. You will also be able to discuss the ideas and issues in the articles.

LISTENING

You will hear authentic interviews with businesspeople and a variety of scripted recordings. You will develop listening skills such as listening for information and note-taking. You can also watch the interviews and find further practice exercises on the DVD-ROM.

LANGUAGE FOCUS

This section focuses on common problem areas at elementary level. You will become more accurate in your use of language. Each unit contains a Language focus box which provides an overview of key grammar items. A Grammar reference section can be found at the back of the book and on the DVD-ROM. The DVD-ROM also provides extra grammar practice.

SKILLS

You will develop essential business communication skills, such as making presentations, taking part in meetings, negotiating, telephoning, and using English in social situations. Each Skills section contains a Useful language box, which provides you with the language you need to carry out the realistic business tasks in the book. The dialogues from the Skills sections appear on the DVD-ROM, which also supplements the Course Book with additional activities.

CASE STUDY

Case studies are linked to the business topics of each unit. They are based on realistic business problems or situations and allow you to use the language and communication skills you have developed while working through the unit. They give you the opportunity to practise your speaking skills in realistic business situations. Each Case study ends with a writing task.

WORKING ACROSS CULTURES

These four units focus on different aspects of international communication. They help to raise your awareness of potential problems or misunderstandings that may arise when doing business with people from different cultures.

REVISION UNITS

Market Leader Elementary third edition also contains four revision units, each based on material covered in the preceding three Course Book units. Each revision unit is designed so that it can be completed in one session or on a unit-by-unit basis.

EXTRA BUSINESS SKILLS

The new Business Skills lessons offer the learner a task-based, integrated skills approach to the development of core business skills such as Presentations, Negotiations, Meetings, and Small Talk. These lessons appear at the end of every three units and incorporate performance review, suggestions for professional development and goal setting. They are based on the Global Scale of English Learning Objectives for Professional English. These objectives are signposted at the top of each new lesson in the Student's book and the carefully scaffolded activities are crafted around each objective, creating a clear sense of direction and progression in a learning environment where learners can reflect on their achievement at the end of the lesson.

Introductions

'James Bond, Universal Exports.'
Sean Connery, British actor, in From Russia With Love

OVERVIEW

VOCABULARY
Nationalities

LISTENING
Meeting business contacts

READING
Angela Ahrendts

LANGUAGE FOCUS 1
to be

LANGUAGE FOCUS 2
a/an with jobs,
wh- questions

SKILLS
Introducing yourself and others

CASE STUDY
A job fair in Singapore

STARTING UP

A Work in pairs. Complete the sentences below with words from the box. There are two words you do not need.

from I'm my name's she you

1 .... Emma. Emma Schneider, from Habermos in Hamburg.

2 Good morning. .... name's Shi Jiabao.

3 My .... Akim, by the way. Akim Anyukov.

4 How do you do. I'm Nuria Sosa, ... RTA Seguros.

B ◀)) CD1.1–1.4 **Now listen to the four businesspeople (1–4) introducing themselves. Check your answers to Exercise A. Match the speakers to their business cards (A–D) on page 7.**

C ◀)) CD1.1–1.4 **Listen again. Where is each speaker? Choose from the following places.**

a) on the phone   b) in a hotel   c) at a conference   d) at the airport

D **Talk about yourself.**

Hello. My name's .... I'm from ....

A ☐

ASTENA Consulting Group

Akim Anyukov
Accountant

PO Box 103
St Petersburg
193015 RUSSIA

Tel: +7 (812) 275-5626
Cell: +7 (812) 101-4046
E-mail: akim@accounts.ru

B ☐

Habermos GmbH

Emma Schneider
Product Manager

Steintwiete 47
20459 Hamburg Germany

Tel: +49 (0) 40-56 91 65 56
Mobile: +49 (0) 177-7 46 94 36
Skype: emmaschneider
E-mail: eschneider@habermos.de

C ☐

RTA Seguros S.A.

Nuria Sosa
Senior Manager

Ayacucho 3813
(B1765ETL) Recoleta
Buenos Aires, Argentina

+(54 11) 4625-1796
E-mail: sosa@rtas.com.ar

D ☐

Shi Jiabao

88 Xue Yuan Road, Hangzhou,
Zhejiang Province, P.R. China 310012

Tel: (0086-571) 2152433
E-mail: jia@mail.zjzs.edu.cn

E 🔊 CD1.5 **Listen to these letters and practise saying them.**

| A H J K | F L M N S X Z | O | R |
| B C D E G P T V | I Y | Q U W | |

F 🔊 CD1.6 **Listen and write the words that are spelled.**

1 .... 2 .... 3 .... 4 ....

G **Work in pairs. Spell the names of some people.**

Student A: Turn to page 130.   Student B: Turn to page 136.

VOCABULARY
Nationalities

A **Complete the chart of countries and nationalities below using the words from the box. Add other countries and nationalities.**

Brazilian Polish Germany Kuwaiti French Oman
Italian Spain Russia Turkey Japanese Swedish
China Greece British American Indian Mexican Korean

Country	Nationality	Country	Nationality
	-an		*-ish*
Brazil	Brazilian	Poland	....
Germany	German	....	Spanish
India	....	Sweden	....
Mexico	....	....	Turkish
Italy	....		*others*
....	Russian	France	....
Korea	....	....	Greek
	-ese	the UK	....
Japan	....	the USA	....
....	Chinese		
	-i		
Kuwait	....		
....	Omani		

B 🔊 CD1.7 **Listen and check your answers to Exercise A.**

C **Work in pairs. Ask and answer questions about the nationality of the companies from the box below.**

Student A: Turn to page 132.

Student B: Turn to page 138.

A: *Is Sony Japanese?*

B: *Yes, it is. Is Chanel Swedish?*

A: *No, it isn't. It's French.*

Sony Chanel Ikea Zara Prada Gazprom Michelin Mercedes McDonald's Samsung Petrobras Tesco Tata Group Telcel

*See the **DVD-ROM** for the i-Glossary.*

D **What are the most famous companies in the world, in your opinion? What is their nationality?**

LISTENING

Meeting business contacts

Jeremy Keeley

A 🔊 CD1.8 **Jeremy Keeley is a consultant. Listen to him introducing himself in the first part of the interview and decide whether these statements are true (T) or false (F). Correct the false ones.**

1 He lives in London.

2 He has three very young children.

3 He runs his own business.

4 His business works for organisations across the USA and Asia.

5 He helps leaders become better leaders.

6 He always shakes hands when he meets people.

*Watch the interview on the **DVD-ROM**.*

B 🔊 CD1.9 **Listen to the second part. Complete what Jeremy says about meeting new business contacts and exchanging business cards.**

I usually say, 'Hello, ...¹ are you?', '............² do you come from?', '............³ do you do?'. I usually find out ....⁴'s important to them, ...⁵ they're there. I usually wait until they've asked me a question before I talk too much about myself.

I usually ....⁶ until the person I'm meeting ....⁷ me a business card before I offer them mine, so we'll ....⁸ them at that point.

C **In business, when do you:**

• shake hands?

• kiss?

• bow?

• exchange business cards?

READING

READING
**Angela
Ahrendts**

A **Read this article. Then complete the chart below.**

From small town to global leader

Angela Ahrendts is the American CEO* of Burberry, the $2.2 billion fashion company. Burberry is one of the biggest luxury brands in the world. The headquarters of this British company are in London, and it has more than 270 stores in 80 countries.

Fifty-year-old Ahrendts is from a small town in Indiana. She is married to Greg, her high-school sweetheart. They have a son (15) and two daughters (14 and 11). Their son, Jennings, dreams of being a rock star. The children are at an American international school in London.

Ahrendts is always elegant. Most days she wears Burberry – usually something from its Prorsum range.

She usually gets up around 4.30. 'I need a quiet time in the morning to answer e-mails,' she explains. On days when Ahrendts is in London, she often has back-to-back meetings for 10 hours. She keeps going by drinking six Diet Cokes a day. She travels on business one week a month, but tries to get home for weekends.

Family is important for Ahrendts. 'I'm at work or with my family. I don't have time for other things.' When she is not working, she likes to eat a takeaway pizza with her children or play basketball with them. Ahrendts and the family go back to Indiana for holidays several times a year. 'We want our children to stay in contact with their cousins,' she says.

* A CEO (chief executive officer) is the person with most authority in a company.

Angela Ahrendts	
Age	50
Job	
Nationality	
Family	
Interests outside work	

B **Decide whether these statements are true (T) or false (F). Correct the false ones.**

1 Burberry is an American company.   *F (It's a British company.)*

2 Burberry is a global fashion company.

3 All Ahrendts's children are teenagers.

4 They are at school in America.

5 Most mornings, Ahrendts is up before 5 a.m.

6 She is away on business most weeks.

7 She has a lot of interests outside work.

8 For Ahrendts, keeping in contact with relatives is important.

C **Work in pairs. Write five questions about Angela Ahrendts and Burberry.**

Is Angela married?

Where is she from?

D **Now work with a different partner. Close your books and ask each other your questions from Exercise C. See who can remember the most answers!**

LANGUAGE FOCUS 1

to be

We often use the verb *to be* to describe people.

Angela Ahrendts **is** *CEO of Burberry. She* **is** *American. She* **is** *married.*

I	am	(I'm)	
You		(You're)	
We	are	(We're)	
They		(They're)	Spanish.
He		(He's)	
She	is	(She's)	
It		(It's)	

I	am not	(I'm not)	
You		(You aren't)	
We	are not	(We aren't)	
They		(They aren't)	Italian.
He		(He isn't)	
She	is not	(She isn't)	
It		(It isn't)	

➡ page 145

A **Complete this information about Maristella with short forms of the verb *to be*.**

My name's......¹ Maristella. I.......² Brazilian and I.......³ from São Paulo. I.......⁴ a research analyst for an investment bank in New York. I.......⁵ married with two children, a boy and a girl. They.......⁶ at high school in Scarsdale. My husband.......⁷ American and he.......⁸ a doctor. My sister.......⁹ in New York, too. She.......¹⁰ a student at Columbia University. We.......¹¹ all interested in sports and movies. My son.......¹² a good tennis player.

B 🔊 **CD1.10 Listen and check your answers.**

C **Complete this chart about yourself. Then introduce yourself to a partner.**

1	Name	....	4	Nationality	....
2	Job	*I'm a(n)*	5	Interests	....
3	City	*I'm from*	6	Favourite sports	....

D **Now write a paragraph about your partner. Use the text in Exercise A as a model.**

My partner's name is ...

E **Complete these sentences with negative forms of *to be*.**

1 She's Russian, but *she isn't* from Moscow.

2 They're Japanese, but .... from Tokyo.

3 He's German, but .... from Munich.

4 I'm in sales, but .... the manager.

5 The office is in Paris, but .... in the centre.

6 Her name is Sophia, but .... Italian.

F Match the questions and answers about Sergio.

1 Are you Spanish?

2 Are you a sales manager?

3 Are you married?

4 Is your wife a manager?

5 Is she Italian?

a) No, I'm a marketing manager.

b) No, she's Mexican.

c) No, I'm Italian.

d) No, she's a lawyer.

e) Yes, I am. That's a picture of my wife.

G Work in pairs. Ask and answer questions about Maristella in Exercise A.

A: *Is Maristella American?*

B: *No, she isn't. She's Brazilian.*

LANGUAGE FOCUS 2

a/an with jobs;
wh- questions

- We use *a* before words beginning with a consonant sound (e.g. *b, c,* etc.):
  a receptionist

- We use *an* before words beginning with a vowel sound (e.g. *a, e,* etc.):
  an architect

- We do not use *a* or *an* with plural nouns:
  They are architects.

- We use question words such as *what, who* and *where* to ask for information:
  'What's your job?' 'I'm *a* lawyer.' (NOT I'm lawyer.)
  'What's your wife's job?' 'She's *an* engineer.'
  'Where's your office?' 'It's in New York.'
  'Who's your boss?' 'Julio Cordón.'
  'Where are you from?' 'I'm Russian.' / **'Where**'s he from?' 'He's Spanish.'

➡ page 145

A Write the correct article (*a/an*) for each job.

accountant   architect   artist   cashier   consultant   director   doctor

engineer   executive   journalist   lawyer   manager   office worker

optician   personal assistant (PA)   pilot   receptionist   research analyst

sales assistant   technician   telephone operator   trainee

B Work in pairs. Talk about your job and the jobs of your family and friends.

I'm a sales manager. My husband/wife/partner is a doctor. My brother is an engineer. My sister is a housewife. My friend is an architect.

C 🔊 CD1.11 –1.13 Listen to three people talking about their jobs and complete this chart.

		Pierre	Gustavo	Silvia
1	What is his/her job?		a lawyer	
2	Where is he/she from?	Switzerland		
3	Where is his/her office?	Singapore		Rome
4	What does his/her partner do?		a journalist	a househusband

D Work in pairs. Ask and answer questions about the three people in Exercise C.

SKILLS

Introducing yourself and others

*Watch the conversations on the **DVD-ROM.***

A ◀)) CD1.14 –1.16 **Listen to three conversations. Decide whether these statements are true (T) or false (F). Correct the false ones.**

CD 1.14

1 Jim Davis works in the advertising department.

2 Paula will be an intern in the company for three weeks.

CD 1.15

3 Lucy Collins works in finance.

4 Jonathan Ross is Jenny Bradshaw's assistant.

CD 1.16

5 Jeff and Susan work for different companies.

6 Jeff's boss is Richard Mason.

B ◀)) CD1.14 –1.16 **Listen again and complete these extracts. Use the Useful language box below to help you.**

CD 1.14

Bob: Hello, Jim. ....^{1} is our new intern, Paula Atkins.

Jim: ....^{2} to meet you, Paula.

CD 1.15

Lucy: Good morning. My ....^{3} Lucy Collins. I'm a finance director. I work for a supermarket group.

Jenny: Hello, I'm Jenny Bradshaw. I'm a ....^{4} of public relations. I work for a big media company.

Lucy: How do you ....^{5}?

Jenny: Nice to meet you.

Lucy: Let me ....^{6} you to my ....^{7}, Jonathan Ross. He's my assistant.

Jonathan: ....^{8} to meet you, Jenny.

CD 1.16

Jeff: Hi, I'm Jeff. I'm ....^{9} Sales.

Susan: Hi, Jeff, I'm Susan. I ....^{10} in Human Resources.

Jeff: How are things ....^{11} in your department?

Susan: Pretty good. I enjoy my work. My ....^{12} are really nice, and I like my boss.

C **Work in pairs or groups of three. Look at the audio scripts of the conversations on pages 158–159. Choose a conversation and practise it.**

D **Work in pairs. You meet over breakfast in a hotel where a business conference is being held. You do not know each other. Role-play the situation. Use phrases from the Useful language box to help you.**

Student A: Turn to page 134.

Student B: Turn to page 140.

USEFUL LANGUAGE

INTRODUCING PEOPLE

I'm … / My name's …

I work for …

This is …

He's/She's in sales / with Nokia.

ASKING QUESTIONS

Where are you from?

What's the reason for your visit?

How's your business doing?

What's the weather like in your country?

Where are you staying?

What's your hotel like?

OFFERING A DRINK

Would you like a drink?

How about a cup of tea / a coffee?

Another drink?

REPLYING

I'm from …

The weather's (quite) good/hot/cold in my country.

I'm staying at [*name of hotel*].

I'm here to [*reason for visit*].

The room is [*describe the room*].

We're doing OK / quite well / very well.

Thanks very much. I'd love one.

Yes, please. / No, thanks.

GREETINGS

How do you do?

Pleased to meet you.

Nice to meet you.

Good to see you again.

SAYING GOODBYE

See you later.

Nice talking to you.

Have a good day.

A job fair in Singapore

A film company is looking for a sales assistant

TREADLIGHT FILM

Background

You and a colleague work for the Treadlight Film Company, a television production company. You are both at a job fair in Singapore. You want to find an assistant for your sales manager in Singapore. On a website, you read information about three young people at the fair looking for a job in sales. Read about them, then do the task below.

Jenny Wong

Age: 20   **Born:** Taiwan
Education: high-school certificate
Work experience: sales assistant in bookshop
Languages: fluent Chinese, basic knowledge of English
Personality/appearance: elegant, friendly
Interests: music, international cinema

Cindy Tan

Age: 21
Born: Hong Kong
Education: university graduate (geography)
Work experience: –
Languages: fluent Chinese, good standard of English
Personality/appearance: well-dressed, confident
Interests: conversation, people

David Chong

Age: 24
Born: Singapore
Education: university graduate (computing)
Work experience: website designer
Languages: fluent Chinese and English
Personality/appearance: serious, hard-working
Interests: computer games, karate

Task

Work in pairs.

1 **Talk about the people in the profiles.**

Jenny Wong is from Taiwan.

She isn't a university graduate.

Cindy Tan has no work experience.

David Chong is interested in computer games.

2 **Imagine you have time to talk to only one of the candidates. Decide which person you want to meet.**

A: I'd like to talk to .... because ....

B: I agree / don't agree. I think ....

3 **You meet at the job fair and talk about the sales position.**

Student A

You are a director of Treadlight Film Company. Ask the job seeker questions based on these prompts:

- Where / you come / from?
- Why / you want / job?
- What / your best quality?
- What / your favourite film or television programme?
- Why / you like the film / television programme?

Student B

You are a job seeker. Think of answers to Student A's questions.

Writing

Write an e-mail to your boss about the person you talked to at the conference.

→ *Writing file page 126*

Hi Bob,

I met an interesting person at a conference in Singapore. Here is some information about him/her …

OVERVIEW

VOCABULARY 1
Days, months, dates

READING
Describing your routine

LANGUAGE FOCUS 1
Present simple

VOCABULARY 2
Leisure activities

LISTENING
Working and relaxing

LANGUAGE FOCUS 2
Adverbs and expressions of frequency

SKILLS
Talking about work and leisure

CASE STUDY
Hudson Design Inc.

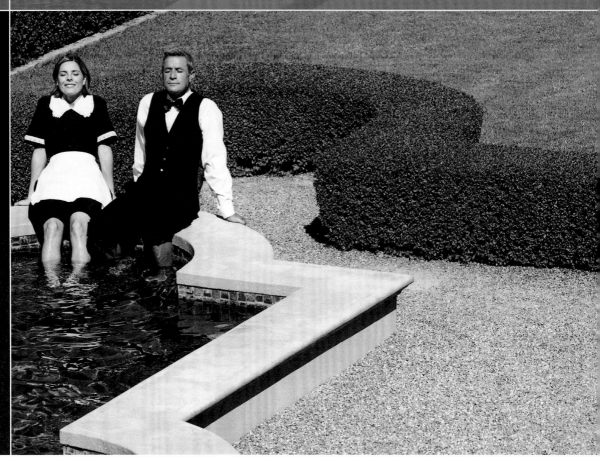

STARTING UP

A **What do people want from work? Discuss in pairs.**

a large office, nice colleagues, ...

B **Work in pairs. Make three word partnerships in each section to find out what four people want from work.**

1	high	colleagues	2	company	phone	3	friendly	security	4	fast	facilities
	long	salary		mobile	facilities		travel	opportunities		flexible	promotion
	helpful	holidays		parking	car		job	boss		sports	hours

🔊 **CD1.17–1.20 Now listen and check the word partnerships they use.**

C **Match six of the word partnerships in Exercise B to their meanings (1–6).**

1 a lot of money   *high salary*

2 a lot of time away from work

3 good people to work with

4 the chance to go to different places on business

5 move quickly to a higher position at work

6 you can change the times when you start and finish work

D **What do *you* want from work? Use the word partnerships from Exercise B and make a list. Work in pairs. Compare your lists and choose the five most important things.**

VOCABULARY 1

Days, months, dates

A **Put the days of the week in order. Which days are 'the weekend'?**

Friday ☐   Monday ☑   Saturday ☐   Tuesday ☐

Sunday ☐   Thursday ☐   Wednesday ☐

B **Write the months of the year under the correct seasons.**

| June April January August December February |
| May October March September November July |

Spring	Summer	Autumn	Winter

C **Complete these time phrases with *in*, *at* or *on*. Then write the phrases under the correct preposition in the table below.**

1 .....*at*..... night

2 .... the autumn

3 .... 15th February

4 .... Thursday

5 .... the afternoon

6 .... Tuesday evening

7 .... June

8 .... New Year

9 .... the weekend

in (x3)	at (x3)	on (x3)
	at night	

D 🔊 CD1.21 **Listen and check your answers to Exercise C.**

E **Complete these sentences with *in*, *at* or *on*.**

1 We have a lot of big orders ....*in*.... March.

2 The office closes for three days .... New Year.

3 There is an important meeting .... 15th June.

4 The CEO visits our branch .... the summer.

5 We deliver large goods .... Monday afternoons.

F **Work in pairs. When are you busy during the day, week and year? What are the quiet times?**

A: When are you busy during the day?

B: I'm very busy in the morning. When are the quiet times for you?

A: Business is quiet in the summer. Which days are you busy during the week?

B: I'm always busy on Mondays.

G **Write about yourself, your company or your school.**

• When are the busy times?

• When are the quiet times?

• Which moments in the year do you particularly enjoy? Why?

*See the **DVD-ROM** for the i-Glossary.*

15

READING
Describing your routine

A **Before you read the article, discuss these questions.**

1 What do you think is a typical day in the life of the CEO of a big company?

2 How much time do CEOs spend travelling?

3 Do CEOs need holidays?

B **Look through this article. Can you find any of the ideas you discussed in Exercise A?**

Business diary: Eugene Kaspersky

by Mary Watkins

Eugene Kaspersky is CEO of Kaspersky Lab, the Russian security software company. The company is based in Moscow and has offices in
5 29 countries. Its main competitor is Symantec. Most of the company's sales are outside Russia.

Kaspersky spends 50% of his time in Moscow, but the other 50% he
10 travels. He is often away for more than three weeks at a time. When he is away, he attends meetings, goes to trade shows and sometimes gives presentations. When he is in the
15 office, he spends time talking informally to colleagues – at their desks or in the company restaurant.

The Moscow office is like a big family. Many people in the
20 office are friends. Some go on holiday together. Everyone dresses informally. Kaspersky normally wears shirts and jeans, but he has a suit for important meetings with
25 presidents and prime ministers.

In Moscow, he does not get up early, especially after a business trip. "On some business trips, I only get three or four hours' sleep a night, so
30 I need to relax," says Kaspersky. At the end of a busy Moscow office day, he goes to the gym with his personal trainer. "It's a great way to relax after a busy day in the office." If he can, he
35 also takes two days off a month.

Holidays are important too. "In winter, I go skiing. In the summer, I often go to the mountains, where I can't use the Internet or my mobile
40 phone. But I can get a satellite connection."

C **Answer these questions.**

1 Is Kaspersky a formal or informal CEO?

2 Is most of his business in Russia or in other countries?

3 Does he work 24/7 (24 hours a day, seven days a week)?

D **Decide whether these statements are true (T) or false (F). Correct the false ones.**

1 Kaspersky travels a lot.   *T*

2 He wears formal business clothes in the office.

3 He gets up early every day.

4 He goes to the gym after work.

5 He likes to have time to relax when he's in Moscow.

6 He only has holidays in summer.

E In each box, match the words that go together.

1	trade	a)	trip
2	business	b)	show
3	personal	c)	day
4	office	d)	trainer

5	attend	e)	presentations
6	give	f)	skiing
7	spend	g)	meetings
8	go	h)	time

F Work in pairs. Tell your partner about your day and your holidays.

I get up …

I arrive at work/school at …

For my holidays, I …

LANGUAGE FOCUS 1
Present simple

- We use the present simple to talk about habits and work routines.
  I **travel** on business.   We **work** long hours.

- We add an **-s** to the verb for *he/she/it*.
  He attend**s** meetings.   She work**s** in Tokyo.

- We use *do* and *does* in negatives and in questions.
  They **don't** work late.   She **doesn't** leave work until *8* p.m.
  Do you drive to work?   **Does** he travel in his job?

➡ page 146

A Darren Throop works for Entertainment One, a media company in Toronto, Canada. Complete the article below about his working day using the verbs from the box.

checks   does   drives   finishes   ~~gets~~   has   likes   makes   spends   travels

Darren Throop …*gets*… [1] up at 6 a.m. and …………[2] some exercise in the gym in his house. At about 6.30, he …………[3] breakfast for his two daughters. Then he …………[4] his e-mails in his home office. He …………[5] to work. At lunch time, he …………[6] a salad at his desk. At work, he …………[7] a lot of time in meetings and on conference calls. He …………[8] his office day at about 5 p.m. He …………[9] on business a lot, so he …………[10] to spend all his free time with his family.

B Complete this information about Masami Kimura. Use the correct form of the verbs in brackets.

I'm Masami Kimura and I'm married with two children, Aiko and Katsuki. They …*go*…[1] (*go*) to an international school. My husband's name is Seito. He …………[2] (*work*) for a shipping company, and I …………[3] (*work*) for an international securities company.

We …………[4] (*live*) in Tokyo, near Shinjuku. I …………[5] (*travel*) to work by subway, but Seito …………[6] (*drive*) to work. We both …………[7] (*like*) sports and travelling. At the weekend, we …………[8] (*play*) golf or we …………[9] (*go*) camping.

C Write a paragraph like the one in Exercise B about yourself.

C 🔊 CD1.38–1.41 **Listen to four phone calls. Match the calls (1–4) to these problems (a–d).**

a) There is a problem with the invoice. ☐

b) The date of the meeting is not suitable. ☐

c) The quantity is not correct. ☐

d) There are no instructions. ☐

D 🔊 CD1.38–1.41 **Listen again and complete these sentences.**

1 I can't meet your ...., Vanessa Gordon, next Wednesday.

2 I'm sure we can .... another time.

3 It's about the .... of mobile phones.

4 Sorry about that. I'll .... with it immediately.

5 There are no .... in the package.

6 Sorry, I didn't .... that. Could you .... it, please?

7 Also, I think the .... are wrong.

8 I'll .... the matter and send you another ....

Watch the phone calls on the DVD-ROM.

E 🔊 CD1.38–1.41 **Look at the Useful language box below. Listen again and tick (✓) the expressions you hear.**

F **Work in pairs. Use these role cards to role-play a conversation. Use some of the expressions from the Useful language box.**

Student A	Student B
Sales Representative	**Customer**
• Answer the phone. • Ask for details. • Apologise for the first problem. • Apologise again and offer solutions. • Say goodbye.	• Introduce yourself. Say you have some problems with an order. • Give details of first problem (ordered grapefruit juice, not orange juice). • Give details of second problem (want 1,000 bottles, not 100 cans, as soon as possible). • Thank the sales representative. • Say goodbye.

USEFUL LANGUAGE

GETTING THROUGH

Can I speak to (Jane Porter), please?

Call me back later, please.

ANSWERING

Hello, this is (Carl Fisher).

Good morning, (David Seymour) speaking.

INTRODUCING YOURSELF

Hello, this is David Patterson, Hudson Motors.

Hello, David Patterson here, Hudson Motors.

STATING THE PROBLEM

I have a problem (with …)

There are some problems with …

APOLOGISING

(Oh dear! I'm) sorry to hear that.

(I'm very) sorry about that.

GETTING DETAILS

Can you give me some more information?

Which model is it?

GIVING DETAILS

The invoice is incorrect.

It's the wrong part/model/item.

There's a piece missing.

FINDING SOLUTIONS

We can give you a refund.

We can send you new ones.

I can talk to the manager.

FINISHING THE CONVERSATION

Thank you.

Thanks for your help. Bye.

High-Style Business Rentals

Are the apartments as good as the adverts say?

Background

High-Style Business Rentals provides apartments for businesspeople who are working abroad. Guests usually want to stay in high-quality apartments which are well furnished and equipped.

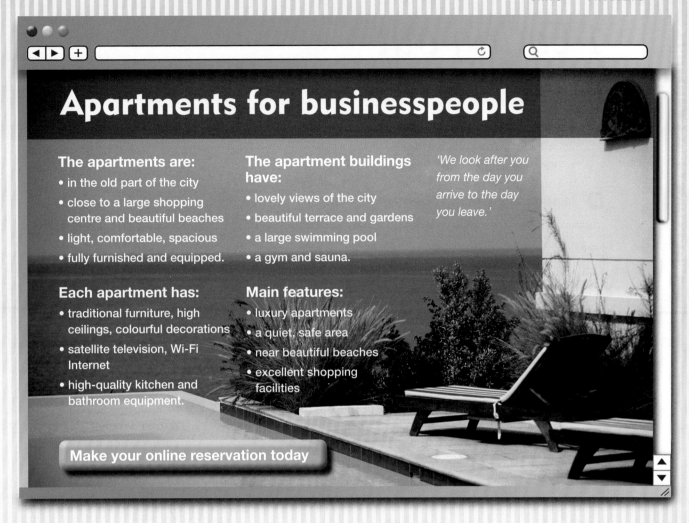

Apartments for businesspeople

The apartments are:
- in the old part of the city
- close to a large shopping centre and beautiful beaches
- light, comfortable, spacious
- fully furnished and equipped.

The apartment buildings have:
- lovely views of the city
- beautiful terrace and gardens
- a large swimming pool
- a gym and sauna.

'We look after you from the day you arrive to the day you leave.'

Each apartment has:
- traditional furniture, high ceilings, colourful decorations
- satellite television, Wi-Fi Internet
- high-quality kitchen and bathroom equipment.

Main features:
- luxury apartments
- a quiet, safe area
- near beautiful beaches
- excellent shopping facilities

Make your online reservation today

🔊 **CD1.42–1.45** Listen to comments from four High-Style guests and make notes.

Task

Work in pairs. You are guests at High-Style Business Rentals.

1 Compare what the online advertisement promises with the guests' experience of the apartments. Say what is different.

The apartments don't have lovely views. The rooms aren't colourful.

2 Student A: See below.   Student B: Turn to page 138.

Read your role cards. Then make the telephone call.

> **Student A**
>
> **Guest at High-Style Business Rentals**
>
> Telephone the company's manager. You are very unhappy with your apartment.
> Tell the manager that you want a:
> - bigger apartment
> - cheaper Internet price ($3 an hour)
> - desk and more chairs in the sitting room
> - new television with satellite programmes.

Writing

You are Diana Nolan, Manager at High-Style Business Rentals.
Write an e-mail to Jason Parker at Head Office.

- Explain the problems you have with High-Style guests.

- Say that you want a meeting with the Director of Marketing.

- Say that you want to discuss High-Style's future advertising policy.

 Writing file page 126

1 Eating out

A In groups, answer these questions.

1 What is your favourite dish?

2 What food don't you like to eat?

3 Have you ever made a mistake when dining? If so, what?

B In pairs, do this quiz. Then check your answers on page 144.

1 In which country is it OK to arrive up to 30 minutes late for dinner?
a) Germany
b) China
c) Italy
d) Denmark

2 In which country is it OK to fill your own glass after you have filled your guest's?
a) the UK
b) Korea
c) Russia
d) Japan

3 In which country is it a good idea to leave some food on your plate?
a) Norway
b) Malaysia
c) Singapore
d) Egypt

4 In which country is chewing gum *not* rude?
a) Luxembourg
b) the USA
c) Singapore
d) Switzerland

5 In Arab cultures, which of these should you avoid when eating?
a) standing up
b) drinking anything
c) using your left hand
d) eating a lot

6 Who usually pays for a business meal in France?
a) the oldest person
b) the host
c) the guest
d) Everyone shares it.

7 In which country is it common to go out to eat after 10 p.m.?
a) Sweden
b) Denmark
c) Austria
d) Spain

8 In which country is interrupting someone during a dinner conversation not rude?
a) Canada
b) Brazil
c) Germany
d) Japan

9 In which country is a strong handshake not good?
a) the USA
b) the UK
c) Germany
d) the Philippines

C ◀)) CD1.46 Listen to the introduction at a workshop on dining. In the first column of this chart, complete the seven topics that the speaker wants to look at.

	Topics	Examples
1		
2		Germany: wait until you are shown where to sit
3		
4	What you use to eat	
5		
6	Body language	Germany: bad to rest your elbows on the table
7		

D ◀)) CD1.46 Listen again and complete the examples in the second column.

Task

1 The Chinese prefer to entertain in public places rather than at home. Look at the notes for guests on the right.

2 Make notes for a short talk giving advice on dining habits for some foreign businesspeople coming to your country or a country you know well. You can use the notes on the right or the headings in the Topics column of the chart in Exercise C to help you.

3 In pairs, give your talks to each other.

- Arrive on time.
- Dress well.
- Greet the eldest person first.
- Learn how to use chopsticks.
- Do not point with your chopsticks.
- Wait to be told where to sit.
- Wait for the host to begin eating first.
- Try everything that is offered to you.

Revision

1 Introductions

Choose the best word to complete each sentence.

1 Mr Dubois lives in Germany, but he comes from *French / France*.

2 Both Aslan and Zeynep are *Turkish / Turkey*.

3 Is JVC a *Japanese / Japan* company?

4 The new accountant is from *Kuwaiti / Kuwait*.

5 What's the capital of *Omani / Oman*?

6 Lloyds isn't *a USA / an American* bank.

7 The company's CEO is *the UK / British*.

8 We manufacture our products at a factory in *China / Chinese*.

9 The company closed its office in *Greece / Greek*.

10 Nokia isn't a *Sweden / Swedish* company!

Complete the conversations below using the words from the box.

'm   'm not   are   are   aren't   is   isn't

A: Where ....^{1} you from?

B: I ....^{2} from Poland – Warsaw. How about you? Are you Chinese?

A: No, I ....^{3}. I come from Japan.

A: ....^{4} your co-workers American?

B: My boss ....^{5} American. He's from New York City. But my other co-workers
............^{6} American. They're French and German.

A: Excuse me. May I use this office for a few minutes?

B: I don't know. It ....^{7} my office. I don't work here. I'm visiting today!

A: Oh, sorry.

Complete these questions with *What, Where* or *Who*.

1 .... is Mr Santos from?   He's from Cuenca, Ecuador.

2 .... is Lenore's job?   She's a manager.

3 .... are you doing?   I'm writing an e-mail.

4 .... is waiting outside?   Mr Jones and three colleagues.

5 .... is the receptionist?   She's in the conference room.

6 .... are you working with?   Ursula and Piet.

2 Work and leisure

Complete these sentences with _in_, _at_ or _on_.

1 The new office opens .... 30th March.

2 All of our shops are open .... night.

3 Can we have a meeting .... Friday?

4 We always have our sales conference .... July.

5 We don't schedule meetings .... Monday mornings.

6 I sometimes work .... the weekend.

7 I usually visit my clients .... the afternoon.

8 I often start new projects .... the spring.

9 We always have a big office celebration .... New Year.

Match the pairs of sentences.

1 He never wakes up before six.

2 He sometimes wakes up before six.

3 He often wakes up before six.

4 He usually wakes up before six.

5 He always wakes up before six.

a) On Mondays and Tuesdays, he wakes up at 5.45. Other days, he wakes up at 6.15.

b) Every day, he wakes up at 5.45.

c) On Mondays, he wakes up at 6.15. Other days, he wakes up at 5.45.

d) On Mondays, Tuesdays and Wednesdays, he wakes up at 5.45. Other days, he wakes up at 6.15.

e) Every day, he wakes up at 6.15.

Put the words in the correct order to make questions.

1 time / What / free / you / in / do / your / do / ?

2 do / finish / you / work / When / ?

3 about / What / like / do / best / you / job / your / ?

4 your / you / in / do / do / job / What / ?

5 Do / colleagues / your / you / after / meet / work / ?

6 work / How / you / hours / many / a / do / week / ?

Write an e-mail (40–60 words) to a new colleague telling them about yourself. Use these topics to help you.

- company/college
- live
- nationality
- enjoy/don't enjoy
- married/single
- work
- hobbies/job
- name

E **Answer these questions.**

1 How far is the hotel from the Shinjuku shopping area?

2 How long is the business centre open?

3 How long does it take to travel from Narita Airport to the hotel?

F **Match the words on the left (1–6) to the words on the right (a–f) to make word partnerships from the text.**

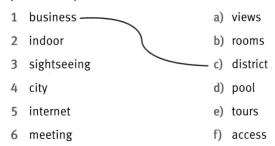

1 business ⎯⎯⎯⎯⎯⎯⎯ a) views

2 indoor b) rooms

3 sightseeing ⎯⎯⎯ c) district

4 city d) pool

5 internet e) tours

6 meeting f) access

LANGUAGE FOCUS 2

there is / there are

- We often use *there is / there are* before *a/an* or *some/any*.
  There is an indoor swimming pool.
  There are three restaurants.
  There aren't any shops in the area.
  '**Are there any** meeting rooms in the hotel?' 'Yes, **there are.**' / 'No, **there aren't.**

➡ page 148

A **Complete these sentences with the correct form of *there is* or *there are*.**

1 It's a very small airport. *There aren't* any shops in the terminal.

2 .... a problem with my ticket?

3 .... any aisle seats available.

4 .... a stopover in Frankfurt.

5 .... any flights to Zurich tonight?

6 I'm afraid .... a flight to Warsaw this afternoon.

7 .... two cafés in the terminal.

8 .... any buses from the airport to the city centre?

B **In pairs, ask and answer questions about the facilities at the Hilton Tokyo.**

A: *Is there a health club?*   B: *Yes, there is.*

B: *How many guest rooms are there?*   A: *There are 808.*

C **Work in pairs. Role-play this situation.**

Student A: See below.   Student B: Turn to page 139.

Student A	
Part 1	**Part 2**
You have a new job abroad. Student B lives there. Ask him/her about these points.	Student B has a new job abroad. You live in that country. Use these notes to answer his/her questions.
• international school?	B: *Are there any good restaurants?*
Is there an international school?	A: *Yes, there are lots of good local restaurants.*
• good local transport?	• No, ... any cinemas.
• big supermarkets?	• Yes, ... lots of good local restaurants.
• houses to rent with gardens?	• No, ... , but you can swim in one of the hotels.
	• Yes, ... tennis club with five courts.

SKILLS

Making bookings and checking arrangements

A 🔊 CD1.62 **Simon is flying to Rome on business. Listen to the phone call and choose the correct answers to these questions.**

1	When is Simon arriving?	⟨Monday⟩ / Wednesday
2	When is he leaving?	Tuesday / Wednesday
3	What kind of room does he want?	single / double
4	How much does the room cost per night?	€120 / €150
5	How many nights is he staying at the hotel?	one night / two nights
6	What time will he arrive?	seven o'clock / six o'clock

B **Work in pairs. Study the Useful language box below. Then role-play the telephone call.**

Student A: You work for the Delta Hotel in Frankfurt, Germany.
Student B: You are a business traveller. You want to book rooms for yourself and a colleague.

A: Answer phone. Give name of hotel.

B: Give your name. Ask for two single rooms with baths from 16th to 20th July.

A: Check booking is for four nights from 16th to 20th July.

B: Price?

A: €150 per night for a single room.

B: Restaurant? Car park?

A: Restaurant: yes
Car park: no
Ask for credit-card details.

B: Visa number: 4921 4456 3714 1009
Expiry date: 12/16

Watch the phone call on the **DVD-ROM.**

C **Work in the same pairs. Study the Useful language box.**

Student A: Turn to page 132.
Student B: Turn to page 136.

Role-play the telephone call.

USEFUL LANGUAGE

RECEPTIONIST / SALES EXECUTIVE

Hello, Capri Hotel / Big Bird Airways. How can I help you?

I can give you a single/double on the first floor.

Is that single (BrE) / one way (AmE) or return (BrE) / round trip (AmE)?

So, that's a single room for two nights, the 4th and 5th.

So, that's a round-trip business-class ticket from London Gatwick to New York?

Can I have your credit-card details, please?

And what are the last three digits of the security number on the back of the card?

What time do you expect to arrive?

Could you repeat that, please?

CALLER

I'd like to book a room from Tuesday the 4th to Thursday the 6th.

I'd like to book two tickets to New York, please.

How much is it per night?

Is there a restaurant in the hotel?

Is there a car park?

Is there a pick-up service?

Can I pay with American Express / MasterCard / Visa?

It's a Visa card. The number is …

The expiry date is …

What time does the flight arrive?

THE GUSTAV CONFERENCE CENTRE

Meeting the needs of different clients

Background

The Gustav Conference Centre is just outside the city centre of Vienna, Austria. Three companies want to stay at the conference centre during the period Friday July 7th to Sunday July 9th.

Read the information about the companies and their needs. Then read the information on the Conference Centre's meeting rooms on page 140.

Company	Number of staff	How long at conference?	Meeting rooms	Seminar rooms
Minnesota Chemicals	80	3 days	1	2 (every day)
Elegant Ways Beauty Products	90	3 days	1	2 (every day)
JooC Designs	35	2 days	1	1 (every day)

Notes

- Minnesota Chemicals is a large international company. It is a new customer for the Conference Centre.
- Elegant Ways Beauty Products and JooC Designs had conferences at the Centre last year.

Other requirements

- Minnesota Chemicals wants: video-conferencing; projector + large screen (5m x 4m), direct access to the terrace and garden
- Elegant Ways Beauty Products wants: video-conferencing; projector + large screen (5m x 4m), direct access to the terrace and garden, technical support
- JooC Designs wants: large screen (5m x 4m), 10 laptops, technical support

🔊 **CD1.63** Listen to the conversation. The conference organiser from JooC Designs makes a request to the Conference Centre. Note down what she wants.

Task

1 Work in pairs. You are the Manager and Assistant Manager of the Conference Centre. Discuss these questions.

   1 Which meeting room do you want to offer company?
   2 What will you say to the conference organiser at JooC Designs?
   3 Is there a problem with the seminar rooms? If so, how can you solve it?

2 The Manager of the Conference Centre telephones the conference organiser of each company. The Manager offers each organiser a meeting and seminar room, and discusses any problems. Role-play the telephone calls. Take turns playing the role of the Manager and conference organiser.

   *We can offer you the ......
   Room. It has a seating
   capacity of 100. There is
   a large screen, but ...*

Writing

You are a receptionist at the Conference Centre. Choose one of the companies and write an e-mail to their conference organiser. Confirm the details of their stay. Include the date of arrival, the date of leaving, the type of meeting room, the number of seminar rooms and some of the room's best features.

→ *Writing file page 126*

STARTING UP

A **What kind of food do/don't you like? Make adjectives from these countries.**

| China Japan Thailand India Turkey Greece Italy |
| France Germany Russia Sweden the UK Spain Mexico |

I like Chinese food. I love Italian food.

B **Match the typical dishes to the adjectives. Then make sentences.**

Curry is an Indian dish.

curry snails sushi spaghetti	American Italian Indian
goulash burger paella	French Mexican Chinese
sweet-and-sour chicken fajitas	Japanese Spanish Hungarian

What other typical dishes do you know?

C **In your country, do businesspeople usually:**

1 have business breakfasts?

2 entertain businesspeople at home?

3 entertain businesspeople at the weekend?

VOCABULARY
Eating out

A **Choose the odd one out in each group of food words below. Use the words from the box to explain your answers.**

fish	fruit	meat	vegetable	seafood

1 salmon   tuna   cod   onion   *onion: It's a kind of vegetable.*

2 beef   apple   lamb   chicken

3 carrots   peas   trout   broccoli

4 veal   grapes   cherries   peaches

5 cabbage   prawns   cauliflower aubergine

~~soup~~ steak pâté

salad   ice cream

grilled fish   fruit

chocolate mousse

spring rolls   tiramisu

cheesecake   pork

roast duck   mutton

prawn cocktail

beef stew   apple pie

stuffed mushrooms

B **Look at these words for parts of a menu. Write the dishes from the box on the left under the correct headings.**

Starter	Main course	Dessert
soup		

C **Think of some unusual food from your country or a country you have visited. How can you describe it?**

It's a kind of ... You have it as a starter / main course / dessert.
You eat it with (potatoes/rice).

D **Choose the correct word to complete each of these sentences.**

1 You ask for the *receipt / menu* at the start of a meal.

2 You ask for the *check / bill* at the end of a meal in London.

3 You ask for the *check / bill* at the end of a meal in New York.

4 You ask for the *tip / receipt* after you pay.

E ◄)) CD1.64 **A man and a woman are ordering a meal in a restaurant. Listen and write *M* for man and *W* for woman.**

1 **Starter**   salad ☐   snails ☐   soup ☑W

2 **Main course**   spaghetti ☐   paella ☐   sushi ☐

3 **Dessert**   ice cream ☐   fruit ☐   apple pie ☐

F **Put these sentences into the order you would hear them during a meal.**

a) You should try the roast duck. It's delicious.   ☐

b) No, thanks. I'm full.   ☐

c) Would you like a starter?   ☐1

d) Right. I'll get the bill.   ☐

e) I'd like the soup, please.   ☐

f) Would you like a dessert?   ☐

g) What do you recommend for the main course?   ☐

h) Thanks very much. That was a lovely meal. I really enjoyed it.   ☐

G ◄)) CD1.65 **Listen and check your answers.**

H **You are in a restaurant.**

Student A: Turn to page 130.
Student B: Turn to page 140.

*See the **DVD-ROM**
for the i-Glossary.*

READING

Fast food in India

A **Discuss these questions in pairs.**

1 How often do you eat in fast-food chains?

2 How popular are they in your country? Who is a typical customer?

3 How do they change their menus for the local market? Give some examples.

B **Do international fast food companies need to change their menus to be successful in India? Read this article to find out.**

FT

India likes fast-food chains

by Amy Kazmin

Busy lives, higher salaries and an increasing number of women at work all mean there is a lot of demand in India for fast food.

5 In India, McDonald's has a lot of fans because of its low prices and vegetarian dishes. At lunchtime, the McDonald's at Mumbai's Phoenix Mills – a big shopping centre – is full 10 of college students, mothers and office workers.

Akshaya Batta, 30, has a quick lunch at McDonald's at least once a week, rather than carry a lunch 15 box from home, as a lot of Indians still do. Sahal Amlani, 30, a store manager, spends Rs50 ($1.10) on an afternoon snack at McDonald's twice a week and takes his family for a 20 McDonald's meal, spending about Rs300 ($6.60) every weekend.

International fast-food companies like McDonald's know how important it is to adapt their food for Indian 25 tastes. They make the menus more spicy and they offer more vegetarian dishes, all at a low price.

In its restaurants, McDonald's does not offer any beef dishes 30 because the mainly Hindu population does not eat beef. Instead, it offers mutton and chicken Maharaja Mac.

Kentucky Fried Chicken (KFC) adapts its chicken dishes for local 35 tastes with the use of Indian spices and cooking techniques. The Pizza Hut menu has a mix of Indian and international dishes. Anup Jain, Director of Marketing for Pizza Hut 40 India, says, "We adapt 20% of our menu for Indian tastes. About 60% of people are vegetarian, so we have a lot more vegetarian toppings on our pizzas."

C **Match the words (1–5) to their meanings (a–e).**

1 salaries
2 demand
3 adapt
4 tastes
5 spicy

a) with a strong and hot flavour
b) the kind of things that someone likes
c) the money people earn for their jobs
d) the need people have for a service
e) change something

D **Read the article again and answer these questions.**

1 What type of customer goes to the Phoenix Mills McDonald's at lunchtime?

2 How many times a week does Akshaya Batta go to McDonald's?

3 How much does Sahal Amlani typically spend in McDonald's at weekends?

4 How do these fast-food companies adapt their menus for Indian customers? Complete these sentences:

a) McDonald's offers ...   b) In its chicken dishes, KFC uses ...   c)   Pizza Hut has ...

5 Why is it necessary to make these changes?

E **Work in pairs. Choose a fast-food chain in your country and decide on two ways to improve it. Think about the design of the restaurant or its menu.**

Share your ideas with another pair.

One idea is to ... Another idea is to ...

LANGUAGE FOCUS 1
some/any

- We use *some* in positive statements.
  *There are **some** very good restaurants in the city centre.*

- We also use *some* when we offer things and ask for things.
  *Would you like **some** more coffee? Can I have **some** tea, please?*

- We use *any* in most questions.
  *Do you have **any** beef?*

- We also use *any* in negative statements.
  *We haven't got **any** beef today.* → page 149

A Tick (✓) the correct sentences. Correct the mistakes in the other sentences.

1 I'd like any water.

   I'd like *some* water.

2 Could I have any more coffee, please?

3 Are there any restaurants near here?

4 There isn't some wine left.

5 I'd like some cheese, please.

6 Do you have any soft drinks?

B Choose the correct words to complete this dialogue.

Mina: There are *some / any*¹ good restaurants in the centre.

Ivan: Yes, but there isn't *some / any*² parking. We could go to the Texas Steakhouse near the airport.

Mina: Do they serve *some / any*³ vegetarian dishes?

Ivan: I don't think so. How about the Marina? They do *some / any*⁴ great fish dishes, and they have *some / any*⁵ vegetarian starters, too.

Mina: Good idea. I'll see if they've got a table for nine o'clock.

LISTENING
Entertaining clients

A ◀)) CD1.66 **Jeremy Keeley is a specialist in change leadership. Listen to the first part of an interview with him. He is talking about how he entertains business contacts and his favourite entertainment. Complete these notes.**

- I like to get to ....¹ my contacts.
- I give them a chance to ....² me about themselves.
- I take them places that we can ....³.
- We walked across a ....⁴ together.
- While we walked, we ....⁵.
- We spent the time talking about what was really ....⁶.

Jeremy Keeley

B ◀)) CD1.67 **Listen to the second part of the interview and decide whether these statements are true (T) or false (F). Correct the false ones.**

1 In restaurants, you should consider noise levels.

2 Sometimes you need to take out clients you don't like.

3 Do not take vegetarians to steak restaurants.

4 You should spend a lot of money entertaining clients.

C **Work in pairs. How would you plan a meal for a mixed group of nationalities?**

Watch the interview on the DVD-ROM.

D ◀)) CD1.68 **Listen to the third part of the interview. Compare your answer in Exercise C to what Jeremy says.**

LANGUAGE FOCUS 2

Countable and uncountable nouns

- Most nouns in English are countable.
  a table, two tables; an apple, two apples

- Some nouns are usually uncountable.
  water, tea, sugar, milk, bread

many*, *much* and *a lot of

- We use *many* with countable nouns in questions and negatives.
  *How **many** hours do you work a week?*
  *I don't go to **many** meetings.*

- We use *much* with uncountable nouns in questions and negatives.
  *How **much** money does she earn?*
  *I don't get **much** time for holidays.*

- We use *a lot of* in all types of sentence.
  *The company has **a lot of** employees.*
  *He doesn't earn **a lot of** money.*
  *Does the company have **a lot of** products?*

➡ page 149

A Tick (✓) the countable nouns.

1	reservation ✓	7	equipment	13	menu	19	transport
2	food	8	hotel	14	money	20	soup
3	air conditioning	9	information	15	overtime	21	work
4	bathroom	10	seat	16	receipt	22	shopping
5	bill	11	luggage	17	dish	23	suitcase
6	employee	12	flight	18	tip	24	leisure

B Correct the mistakes in these sentences. Use *a lot of*, *many* or *much*.

1 They don't have ~~much~~ vegetarian dishes here. *a lot of / many*

2 How many does it cost?

3 The restaurant hasn't got much tables left.

4 I don't have many time at the moment.

5 I drink much coffee.

6 There aren't much hotels in the city centre.

7 It costs much money.

8 I don't want many spaghetti. There's ice cream for dessert.

C Work in pairs. Complete these questions with *many* or *much*. Then ask and answer the questions with a partner.

1 A: How *much* cash do you have in your wallet?

   B: *About 20 euros.*

2 How .... phone calls do you make a day?

3 How .... people are there in your company?

4 How .... time do you have for lunch?

5 How .... holiday do you get a year?

6 How .... languages do you speak?

7 How .... fast-food restaurants are there where you live?

8 How .... water do you drink a day?

SKILLS

Making decisions

A What can businesspeople do to entertain a group of visitors? Which of these do you think are a good idea?

- eating local food
- watching a sports match
- eating international food
- going on a tour of the area
- seeing a show (e.g. at the theatre)
- visiting a local sight (e.g. a museum or art gallery)

B ◀》 CD1.69 Two managers are discussing how to entertain a group of important foreign visitors. Listen and decide whether these statements are true (T) or false (F). Correct the false ones.

1 They both like the idea of visiting the castle.

2 They talk about three different restaurants.

3 They decide to go to an Italian restaurant.

4 The table is for 10 people on Tuesday.

C ◀》 CD1.69 Listen again and complete these extracts.

1 I don't .... about that. I think we .... something more interesting for them to do.

2 Yes, I .... I also .... it's too far away. Why .... we invite them for dinner?

3 Good .... Which restaurant do you recommend?

4 We .... try the new restaurant at the Grand Hotel. It's very popular.

5 Yes, that's right, ... it's very expensive!

6 How .... a restaurant by the river?

7 Yes, that's a .... idea.

*Watch the discussion on the **DVD-ROM**.*

D Find examples in Exercise C of these functions.

a) giving opinions   c) disagreeing

b) agreeing   d) making suggestions

E Role play. Work in groups of three. You are managers in a company. You meet to discuss how to entertain a group of six foreign visitors.

Student A: Turn to page 134.
Student B: Turn to page 136.
Student C: Turn to page 143.

F Meet together and discuss your ideas. Decide on the best way to entertain the visitors.

USEFUL LANGUAGE

SUGGESTING

Why don't we visit an art gallery?

How about (trying) the Mexican restaurant?

My suggestion is to go for a cocktail.

Let's go to the new French restaurant.

GIVING OPINIONS

I think Lucio's is the best restaurant. The food is delicious.

We need to go to the Chinese restaurant. It's close to the office.

In my opinion, an Indian curry is the best idea.

For me, a typical Spanish evening is a great idea.

AGREEING

Yes, exactly, because it's easy to get a large table.

Yes, I agree. It's very easy to find.

That's true. There's a nice view of the lake.

Yes, that's a great idea.

You're right. The food is great.

DISAGREEING

I see what you mean, but I don't think we have time.

I don't know about that. I think it's too far away.

That's right, but it's not cheap.

That's a good point, but you need to book/reserve.

Which restaurant?

Choosing the right place for guests

Background

You work for a food company, Organic 3000, in Sydney, Australia. Four important overseas customers are visiting your head office. You want to take them to a good restaurant. Each customer prefers a different type of food. You have three restaurants to choose from.

PACO AND ROSITA
MEXICAN RESTAURANT

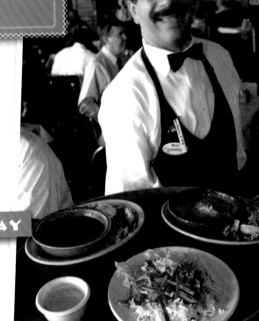

A popular place. High-quality food, good value for money. No reservations, so you often wait a long time for a table.

Location:	In the city-centre restaurant area, close to office and hotels
Access:	By bus or car; difficult to find parking spaces
Atmosphere:	Lively, noisy, loud music
Average cost:	$40 per person

ON THE MENU

- Hot, spicy Mexican dishes
- Grilled steak, pork and chicken
- Not many vegetarian dishes
- No desserts

WHAT PEOPLE SAY

- Delicious meals at low prices
- Very friendly but slow service

Kerala Sands
South Indian Restaurant

Delicious food. Many Indian customers. It isn't near the centre and is expensive.

Location:	5 miles from the city centre
Access:	By car; lots of parking spaces
Atmosphere:	Very quiet; no music
Average cost:	$70 per person

on the menu

- A variety of South Indian dishes
- Vegetable curries
- Well-known dish: prawns with garlic and cabbage
- Many desserts

what people say

- High-quality food and service
- Not much atmosphere
- Food portions rather small

THE
Happy Lobster

Top-class food. Varied fish and seafood dishes.
The restaurant is mentioned in all the guide books.

Location:

2 miles from city centre; on the shore; wonderful view of the bay and city at night

Access:

About half an hour by boat, 20 minutes by car; parking available

Atmosphere:

Quiet; classical music playing all the time

Average cost:

$120 per person

On the menu

- Prawns, crab and oysters. It is famous for its giant crab with spring onions
- Vegetarian dishes
- A few beef and pork dishes
- Delicious desserts

What people say

- Good food, but very expensive
- Usually a long wait for service and the bill
- Very quiet atmosphere

Task

1 **Work in groups of four. Choose a role card. Each of you has information about one of the customers.**

Student A: Turn to page 132. Student C: Turn to page 141.
Student B: Turn to page 139. Student D: Turn to page 142.

2 **Read your role cards. Then exchange information about the customers. Take notes on their preferences and the things they dislike.**

3 **Choose *one* of the restaurants to take the four customers for a meal. Compare your choice with the other groups.**

Writing

Write an e-mail to one of the customers. Invite him or her to dinner and give details of the restaurant. Include the date and time, and the name, location and type of restaurant.

Dear …
I would like to invite you for a meal on …

→ *Writing file* page 126

UNIT

6 Buying and selling

'I buy when other people are selling.'
J. Paul Getty (1892–1976), US entrepreneur, oil-industry executive and financier

STARTING UP

A What was the last thing you bought? Where did you buy it? What do you buy online?

B 🔊 CD1.70–1.72 Listen to three people talking about the products they buy. Where and when do they buy them? Complete this chart.

Speaker	Product	Place	How often
1		on the Internet	
2			once a year
3			

C Where do you buy the products in Exercise B? How often do you buy them? Use the words from the box.

I buy clothes in high-street stores. I usually buy something every month.

usually   once a week   at the weekend   sometimes   every day

D Work in pairs. Choose two other products you buy. Talk about where and how often you buy them.

E Is there a product you prefer *not* to buy online? Why?

VOCABULARY 1
Choosing a product

A Read the Elise sales advert below and find expressions which mean the following.

1 There are some good offers. *great deals*

2 The buyer pays only a small amount of money at the beginning.

3 The buyer pays some money every four weeks for a year.

4 There is no cost for transporting the goods to the buyer.

5 It doesn't cost extra to pay over **12** months.

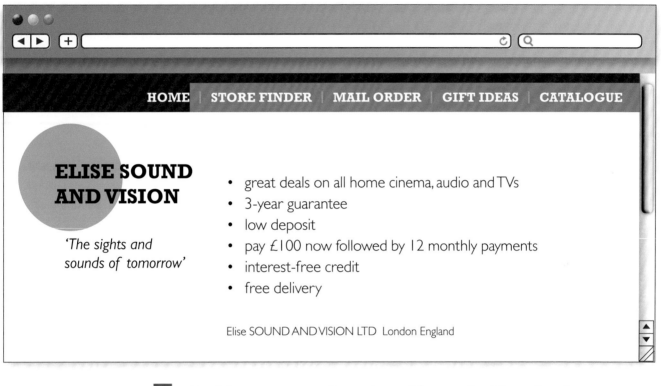

HOME | STORE FINDER | MAIL ORDER | GIFT IDEAS | CATALOGUE

ELISE SOUND AND VISION

'The sights and sounds of tomorrow'

• great deals on all home cinema, audio and TVs
• 3-year guarantee
• low deposit
• pay £100 now followed by 12 monthly payments
• interest-free credit
• free delivery

Elise SOUND AND VISION LTD London England

B Read these sentences. Does a buyer (B) or a seller (S) say them?

1 We offer great deals. ☑ S
2 I'd like to place an order. ☐
3 Do you give a guarantee? ☐
4 I'd like to compare prices. ☐
5 Are the goods in stock? ☐
6 Can you pay a deposit? ☐
7 We always deliver on time. ☐
8 Can I make monthly payments? ☐

C ◀)) CD1.73 Listen to a conversation between a buyer and a seller. Underline the correct answers to these questions.

1 Which model does Karl want? PS**7** / TX**7**
2 How long is the guarantee? three years / two years
3 How much deposit is needed for large orders? **15%** / **10%**
4 What does the seller say is a large order? over **50** units / over **25** units
5 Does the seller always have goods in stock? yes / no

D What is important for you when you buy a product like a computer, TV or car? Put these items in order of importance.

• a three-year guarantee
• interest-free credit
• a low deposit
• free delivery
• a big discount
• great after-sales service

*See the **DVD-ROM** for the i-Glossary.*

READING
A success story

A Before you read the article below, discuss these questions.

1 What global fashion companies do you know?

2 Which are the most successful in your country?

3 What do you know about Uniqlo, the global fashion retailer?

B Match these words (1–6) to their meanings (a–f).

1 expansion
2 strategy
3 relaunch
4 flagship store
5 hire
6 collection

a) employ someone to do a job
b) when something gets bigger in size
c) clothes produced by a designer for the season
d) introduce something new again
e) a detailed plan for achieving something
f) a company's main store, often big and in an important shopping area

C Read the article quickly and underline these numbers and dates. Then say what they refer to.

1 1984   2 2003   3 2005   4 November 2006   5 April 2009   6 ¥49.8 bn   7 64

Uniqlo: a global success story

Tadashoi Yani, the founder of Uniqlo, is Japan's richest man. That's not bad for someone who started with a single store in Hiroshima in 1984 and now has a global retail business. The company sells high-quality casual clothes at low prices.

Uniqlo grew quickly in Japan during the 1990s. In 1998, it had over 300 stores. Following the good results in Japan, Yani decided on global expansion. It started with stores in the UK in 2001. It didn't work. Most of the stores were too small and in the suburbs of cities. In 2003, Uniqlo closed most of them. In 2005, Yani changed strategy. The new strategy was to open large stores in major cities around the world. The relaunch of Uniqlo began in November 2006 with the opening of a flagship store in New York. Over the next two years, the number of international stores went up from 54 to 92, including flagship stores in London and Paris.

Yani also hired the German designer Jil Sander in April 2009. Her role was to design a collection for Uniqlo and to be the creative consultant for the company. The collection went on sale in selected stores in March 2010. In 2010, Uniqlo made profits of ¥49.8 bn.

Yani sees Asia as a key market for Uniqlo. In 2007, the company had 26 stores across Asia. The number increased to 64 at the end of 2010, including a flagship store in Shanghai. Yani's plan is for another 500 stores over the next five years, mainly in China. Yani also aims to introduce Uniqlo stores in the fast-growing Indian and Brazilian markets.

D Decide whether these statements are true (T) or false (F). Correct the false ones.

1 In the 1990s, Japan was Uniqlo's main market.

2 Uniqlo had a lot of success when it entered the UK market in 2001.

3 Yani's new global strategy was to open big stores in important cities.

4 At the end of 2008, Uniqlo had 92 international stores.

5 Yani hired Jil Sander to design all Uniqlo's clothes.

6 Uniqlo opened 64 stores in Asia between 2007 and 2010.

E **Look through the article and find the missing verbs.**

1 Uniqlo .... quickly in Japan during the 1990s.

2 Over the next two years, the number of international stores .... from 54 to 92.

3 The number (of stores) .... to 64 at the end of 2010.

What do the verbs have in common?

F **What makes a business successful? Put these points in order for you. Add other points to the list.**

- ability to learn from mistakes
- hard work
- luck

- money
- personal contacts
- having clear strategy and plan

LANGUAGE FOCUS 1
Past simple

- We use the past simple to talk about completed actions in the past.
  *Last year, we **increased** our sales by 15 per cent.*

- We usually form the past simple by adding *-d* or *-ed* to the verb.
  save – saved   launch – launched   export – exported

- About 150 irregular verbs form the past simple differently.
  cost – cost   be – was – were   grow – grew
  spend – spent   give – gave   go – went

For a list of the most common irregular verbs, see page 157.   ➡ page 150

A ◀)) CD1.74 **Listen to how the *-ed* endings of these verbs are pronounced.**

1 saved; delivered /d/   2 launched; worked /t/   3 decided; visited /ɪd/

B ◀)) CD1.75 **Listen and put these verbs into the correct group from Exercise A (1, 2 or 3).**

| started   finished   advised   lived   wanted   opened   missed   booked   invited |

◀)) CD1.75 **Listen again and practise saying the verbs.**

C **Complete this sales report. Use the past simple of the verbs in brackets.**

Report on sales trip – South Korea

Last December, I visited [1] (*visit*) our major customers from big department stores in South Korea.

I ....[2] (*arrive*) in Seoul on Monday 5th December. The next day, I ....[3] (*meet*) Mrs Kyoung Ai Lee in Seoul. On 7th December, I ....[4] (*make*) a presentation to Mrs Lee's sales staff on our products and ....[5] (*advise*) them how to display them.

The following day, I ....[6] (*go*) to Busan, and our agent ....[7] (*introduce*) me to Mrs Ha, the chief buyer of a new department store in the city. She ....[8] (*ask*) me to send her 500 brochures. I ....[9] (*give*) her some samples of our products.

I ....[10] (*fly*) back to head office in Paris on 9th December.

D **Work in pairs. Take turns to describe a trip you made for business or pleasure.**

E SPEAKING 2

Work in pairs. Take turn to present information about another conference centre. Listen to your partner, take notes and give feedback.

Student A: Turn to page vi.

Student B: Turn to page viii.

F LISTENING 3

◀» **BSA2.2.11 Listen to the question and answer session at the end of the presentation. Complete the sentences with the words you hear.**

1 A: What about parking?

   B: James, ... you .... this?

2 A: .... restaurants?

   B: Do you .... in Orlando?

3 A: .... the cost of entertainment be included?

Task

Pre-task: Research

Context: You work for an international company looking for a suitable conference centre for a training meeting.

Work in two groups, A and B. You are going to give a group presentation about one of the conference centres on page vii. Read the information and make notes.

Part 1: Preparation

1 **In your groups, prepare a 3–4 minute presentation. Decide who will speak in each section of the presentation. Think about the presentation structure, techniques and language.**

2 **Complete the gaps using phrases from Exercises A and C4.**

Structure:

- **Introducing the presentation:** Who are you? Why are you giving the presentation? What are you going to talk about?

- **Main part of the presentation:** Give the main factual information about the centre: location, travel, facilities, food and entertainment.

- **Ending:** What main points do you need to repeat?

Techniques and language:

- Speak ....[1] and ....[2] at the audience.
- Use this phrase to introduce another speaker and explain what they are going to talk about ....[3].

- Use these phrases to introduce a new point. ....[4], ...[5], ...[6], ...[7].

Part 2: Presentation

Take turns to give your presentations in groups.

Presenters: Use the structure in Part 1. Give your presentation.

Audience: Make notes on the key information while you listen. Think of one question to ask.

G PEER REVIEW

Complete the sentences about another presentation. Give feedback.

You covered these things in the main part of your presentation:

....

....

You used these techniques / this language when presenting:

....

....

One thing you did very well was ....

One suggestion to improve your presentation is ....

H SELF-ASSESSMENT

Look back at the lesson objectives. Complete the sentences.

I can ....

I can't ....

I PROFESSIONAL DEVELOPMENT AND PERFORMANCE GOALS

What information do you need to present in your job? Write three sentences about how you could use the skills in this lesson.

1 ....

2 ....

3 ....

'*A company is only as good as the people it keeps.*'
Mary Kay Ash (1918–2001), US businesswoman (founder of Mary Kay Cosmetics)

STARTING UP

A **Work in pairs. Take it in turns to ask each other these questions, then write the answers in the chart on the left.**

Me	My partner
1	1 ....
2	2 ....
3	3 ....
4	4 ....
5	5 ....
6	6 ....
7	7 ....
8	8 ....

1 Do you like to work ...

   a) alone?   b) in a team?   c) with a partner?

2 For appointments, do you like to be ...

   a) early?   b) on time?   c) five minutes late?

3 Do you prefer to work ...

   a) at home?   b) in an office?   c) outside?

4 Do you like to travel ...

   a) to new places?   b) to places you know well?   c) only when you need to?

5 In meetings, do you prefer ...

   a) not to speak much?   b) to speak a lot?   c) to be the chairperson?

6 When do you work best?

   a) In the morning   b) In the afternoon   c) In the evening or at night

7 Do you think a lot about the ...

   a) future?   b) past?   c) present?

8 Do you like your friends or colleagues to be ...

   a) intelligent?   b) good-looking?   c) funny?

B **Work in new pairs. Tell each other about your own and your first partner's answers.**

I like to work in a team. Selim likes to work in a team, too. Selim likes to be on time for appointments, but I like to be early.

VOCABULARY

VOCABULARY
Describing people

A Match the statements (1–10) to the adjectives (a–j).

They …

1 like to spend time with other people.
2 want to reach the top in their career.
3 have a lot of new ideas.
4 do what they promise to do.
5 are usually calm.
6 spend a lot of time doing a good job.
7 like to be on time.
8 encourage other people to work well.
9 are good at making things work.
10 like to do things for other people.

They are …

a) ambitious.
b) creative.
c) hard-working.
d) motivating.
e) helpful.
f) punctual.
g) relaxed.
h) sociable.
i) practical.
j) reliable.

B Use adjectives from Exercise A to complete this human-resources report.

Maria Karlsson

Maria is good in a team and she gets on well with her colleagues. She is extremely *sociable*[1]. She is never late for meetings – she is always ....[2]. She is very ....[3]; she always meets deadlines. She is in the office at 8.00 a.m. every day and usually stays late, so she is very ....[4]. Her boss says this is very ....[5] to others. Her colleagues have a lot of respect for her work and attitude.

She is also a very ....[6] person with a lot of good ideas for the future of the company.

C Look again at the adjectives in Exercise A. Which do you think are the three most important for a) a boss; b) a colleague in a team? Discuss your answers with a partner.

*See the **DVD-ROM** for the i-Glossary.*

I think a hard-working boss is important.

I like to work with ambitious people. They give me energy.

LISTENING

LISTENING
Managing people

A 🔊 CD2.1 Ros Pomeroy, a management consultant, talks about the people she likes to work with. Listen to the first part of the interview. Which adjectives from Vocabulary Exercise A does she mention?

B 🔊 CD2.2 Listen to the second part of the interview and answer these questions.

1 Why did team members hide information from one bad manager?
2 Why were the team members not prepared to take any risks?

Ros Pomeroy

C 🔊 CD2.3 Listen and complete the final part of the interview.

Well, luckily, I have met and worked with several good managers, and these are people who are willing to delegate; that is, they will give a ....[1] to a team member to get on and ....[2]. They are less ....[3] in how a task is done, but they are clear about setting the ....[4] and being clear about what ....[5] they expect.

And a good manager will also give ....[6] and ....[7] to a team member when they do a good job.

*Watch the interview on the **DVD-ROM**.*

D Answer these questions in pairs.

1 What kind of people do you like working with?
2 What kind of people do you not like working with?

LANGUAGE FOCUS 1

Past simple: negatives and questions

- For negatives and questions in the past simple, we use the auxiliary *did* (*didn't*) and the infinitive form of the verb.
  You **didn't like** your colleague.
  Did he **leave** the company?
  Why **did** he **leave** the company?

- Note the form with the verb *to be*.
  He **wasn't** good at his job.
  They **weren't** happy at work.
  Was Dan efficient?
  When **were** they in France?

➡ page 151

A **Put these words in the right order to make sentences about problems at work.**

1 the deadlines / the projects / weren't / for / realistic
  The deadlines for the projects weren't realistic.

2 most people / the office / didn't / leave / until 8 p.m.

3 a / manager / good / wasn't / she

4 on time / start / meetings / didn't

5 didn't / she / to motivate / know / the staff / how

B 🔊 CD2.4 **Listen to a conversation to check your answers.**

C **Correct one mistake in each line of this message.**

Maris, I'm sorry. I'm having a bad day. I didn't ~~sent~~ the report
out, and I not check the figures. I didn't get to the bank
on time, and I didn't phoned the suppliers. I tried to call you
this morning, but you not answer. I think I need to go home.

1 ...*send*...
2 ....
3 ....
4 ....

D **Complete these questions with *did*, *was* or *were*.**

1 ...*Was*... he an efficient manger?

2 When .... you born?

3 When .... Ania start to work for IBM?

4 Why .... Marcus change jobs?

5 Where .... your next job?

E **Read the extract below. Then write questions using each of the words from the box.**

Where did Danielle grow up?

| Why   How long   What   When   Where |

Danielle grew up in Geneva. She studied engineering at university in Paris.
Then she worked for Renault for four years, from 2004 until 2008. She left Renault
because she wanted to do an MBA. She did an MBA at the Harvard Business School
in 2009. Her next job was with GE.

F **Work in pairs. Ask your partner questions about his/her past studies and/or jobs.**

READING
Andrea Jung

A Before you read the article below, discuss these questions.

1 What famous businesswomen do you know?

2 What qualities do you need to be a successful business executive?

Andrea Jung

- Born in:
  ....

- Grew up in:
  ....

- Education:
  ....

- Appearance:
  ....

- Company:
  ....

- Professional
  achievements:
  ....

B As you read the article, make quick notes to complete the profile of Andrea Jung on the left.

C Decide whether these statements are true (T) or false (F). Correct the false ones.

1 Avon sells cosmetics through shops.

2 Andrea Jung speaks English and Chinese.

3 Around 50 per cent of managers at Avon are women.

4 Avon has an all-female board.

5 Jung thinks all-women management teams make the best decisions.

6 She is on the boards of two other companies.

D Find words or phrases in the article with these meanings.

1 people who sell a company's products (paragraph 1)

2 when you decide to do something and do not let anything stop you (paragraph 3)

3 leave a job without finishing it (paragraph 3)

4 all the money that a company receives regularly (paragraph 4)

5 a very strong liking for something (paragraph 6)

E Work in pairs. Imagine you are going to interview Andrea Jung. Write five questions that you would like to ask her.

FT

Women at the top: Andrea Jung

1 In 2011, Andrea Jung celebrated 12 years as Chief Executive of Avon Products. It is a big job. Avon sells cosmetics door to door in more than 120 countries. It has 6.2m sales representatives and a billion customers. It sells four lipsticks and 190 mascaras every second.

2 Jung was born in Toronto to Chinese immigrant parents. Her parents moved to the US when she was two, to get a better education for their children. She grew up in Massachusetts and graduated from Princeton. She speaks fluent Mandarin.

3 "My parents were important in forming my views about leadership," she says. Determination is a strong quality in Chinese culture. In her early career, she had a job that wasn't interesting. She told her parents she didn't like the job and wanted to quit. "'Quit?' they said. 'The Chinese don?t quit. You learn more from bad than good experiences – that's how you grow.'"

4 Jung joined Avon in 1994. Four years later, she became Avon's first female CEO. At that time, the company had revenues of $4bn. Today, its revenues are more than $10bn.

5 Avon is known as "the company for women". Most of Avon's representatives are women. About half the managers and four out of the nine members of Avon's board are women. Jung says there are good business reasons for management teams with a mix of men and women. "In mixed teams, communication and

decision-making are better."

6 Famous for her long black hair, pearl necklaces and her passion for Avon, Jung is one of the world's top business leaders. She is also on the board of GE and Apple.

Question forms

- We form questions which can be answered with *yes* or *no* in two ways.

With *be* or a modal verb (e.g. *can*)	Form of *be* / modal verb	Subject	
He is ambitious.	**Is**	he	ambitious?
She can see us now.	**Can**	she	**see** us now?

With all other verbs	Form of *do* (or other auxiliary)	Subject	
Ana likes Madrid.	**Does**	Ana	**like** Madrid?
Joe left the company.	**Did**	Joe	**leave** the company?

- We begin other types of question with a question word such as *why, where, when, how,* etc.

	Question word	Form of *do, be,* modal or auxiliary	Subject	
She works hard.	Why	**does**	she	**work** hard?
He went away.	When	**did**	he	**go** away?
They were stressed.	Why	**were**	they	stressed?

➡ page 151

A **Discuss these questions in pairs.**

1 What was Steve Jobs's greatest success?

2 What made him successful?

B **Read this article (ignoring the missing information), then write the questions to complete the quiz on page 71. Use the article to help you.**

Barack Obama described Steve Jobs as 'one of the greatest American innovators'. This is his story. He was born on February 24, 1955, ...[1]. In 1976, after dropping out of college, Jobs started Apple with ....[2]. The company quickly became successful. In ....[3], Apple introduced the famous Macintosh computer. The following year, in 1985, Jobs left Apple because of ....[4].

After leaving Apple, Jobs set up a new computer company called NeXT. He also bought a company called Pixar. It specialised in ....[5].

Jobs married his wife, ...,[6] at a Zen Buddhist ceremony in 1991. The couple had three children.

The early nineties were difficult years for Apple, and the company soon wanted Jobs back. In December 1996, Apple bought Jobs's company NeXT. Apple paid ....[7] for it. Jobs returned to Apple and in 1997 became the CEO. Under his leadership, Jobs turned the company around, with innovative products such as the iMac, iPod, iPhone and iPad. In ....[8], after a long period of illness, Steve Jobs resigned as Apple's CEO. He died two months later at the age of ....[9]. ....[10] is Apple's new CEO.

In his time at Apple, Steve Jobs created the most valuable technology company in the world. Today, it employs more than ....[11] people worldwide.

1 *Where was Steve Jobs born?*
- a) In California
- b) In Portland, Oregon
- c) In Chicago

2 ....?
- a) A manager at Hewlett Packard
- b) His father
- c) His friend Steve Wozniak.

3 ....?
- a) In 1980
- b) In 1982
- c) In 1984

4 ....?
Because of ...
- a) bad health.
- b) a great job offer.
- c) disagreements with the CEO, John Sculley.

5 ....?
- a) Music
- b) Computer animation
- c) Computer software

6 ....?
- a) Melinda
- b) Patricia
- c) Laurene

7 ....?
- a) $400m   b) $200m   c) $600m

8 ....?
- a) March 2011
- b) August 2011
- c) October 2011

9 ....?
- a) 50   b) 56   c) 65

10 ....?
- a) Tim Cook
- b) Jonathan Ive
- c) Phil Schiller

11 ....?
More than ...
- a) 20,000.
- b) 57,000.
- c) 46,500.

C ◀)) CD2.5 **Listen and check the questions you wrote.**

D **Answer the questions in the quiz above and use your answers to complete the article on page 70.**

E ◀)) CD2.6 **Now listen and check your answers.**

F **Work in pairs. Take it in turns to choose five questions from the quiz and 'test' your partner. Help with answers if necessary.**

G **Complete these sentences. Give true information about yourself.**

1 Last year, I bought *a new camera.*

2 Yesterday, I was ...

3 Last summer, I ...

4 When I was a child, ...

H **Work in pairs. Tell each other your true sentences. Ask as many follow-up questions as you can.**

A: *Last year, I bought a new camera.*

B: *Really! What make was it? / Where did you buy it? / How much did it cost?*

SKILLS

Dealing with problems

A **Work in pairs. Discuss which of these suggestions you agree with.**

When two people try to solve a problem, it is a good idea for them to:

1 describe the problem in detail.

2 show strong feelings.

3 give reasons if they have to say no.

4 speak quietly.

5 find a solution immediately.

B 🔊 CD2.7 **Julian works for a coffee importing company. He is talking to the Office Manager, Hanna Butler. Listen and answer these questions.**

1 What does Julian want the company to do?

2 What does Hanna suggest to solve the problem?

3 Does Hanna offer to give Julian any money?

C 🔊 CD2.7 **Listen again and complete these extracts.**

Hanna: Look, I'm really ....¹ , Julian. The ....² is, we don't have enough money to pay for language courses.

Hanna: I'm sorry, Julian – it's just not ....³ . Why don't you buy one of those self-study courses in Spanish? They're ....⁴, and you can improve your Spanish a lot if you study ....⁵.

Julian: OK, I'll do that. Will the company ....⁶ for a self-study course if I buy one?

Hanna: I can't ....⁷ anything, Julian. But bring the ....⁸ to me and I'll see what I can do for you.

D **Which of the suggestions in Exercise A do Hanna and Julian follow?**

Watch the discussion on the DVD-ROM.

E **Work in pairs. An office worker in a car-hire firm wants to start work later in the morning, but the manager does not agree. Role-play the situation.**

Student A: Turn to page 131.
Student B: Turn to page 139.

USEFUL LANGUAGE

EMPLOYEE

Describing the problem ────────────▶

I need some training to do my job properly.

I don't have enough money to pay for classes.

Emphasising the problem ───────────▶

It's really important for me.

It would be really helpful to me.

MANAGER

Making suggestions ──────────────▶

Why don't you buy a self-study course?

How about studying at home?

Giving advice

I think you should visit the shopping centre.

MANAGER

Responding

I'm sorry. It's just not possible.

Explaining the reasons

The problem is, we don't have the money for this.

You see, we have to cut costs.

EMPLOYEE

Accepting suggestions or advice

OK, I'll take a look at one.

OK, I'll think about it.

Tell us about it

Office workers share their problems and offer solutions

Background

A magazine, *Business Today*, has a message board on its website called Office Life.
People who have problems at work can leave messages there, either online or by
phone. Readers comment on the problems and give advice about how to solve them.
Read the problems and discuss the questions below.

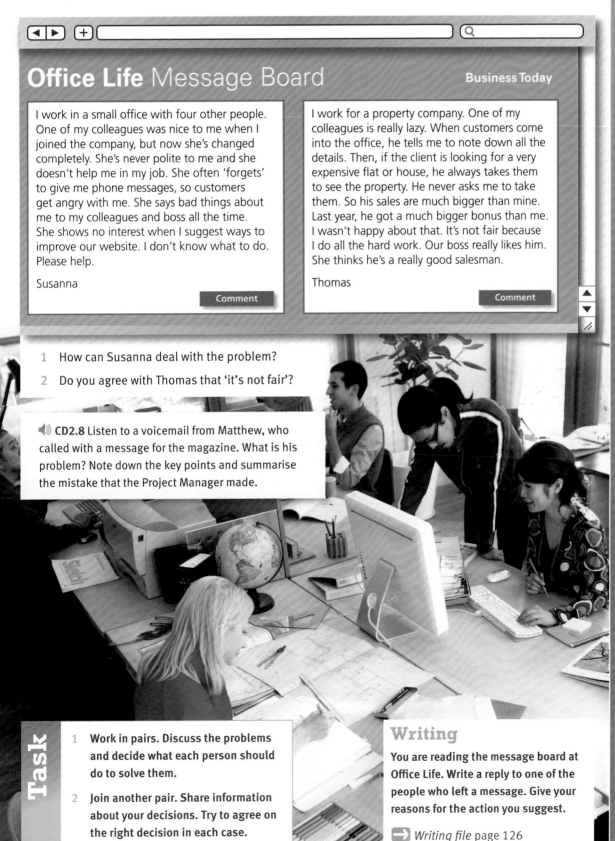

Office Life Message Board

Business Today

I work in a small office with four other people.
One of my colleagues was nice to me when I
joined the company, but now she's changed
completely. She's never polite to me and she
doesn't help me in my job. She often 'forgets'
to give me phone messages, so customers
get angry with me. She says bad things about
me to my colleagues and boss all the time.
She shows no interest when I suggest ways to
improve our website. I don't know what to do.
Please help.

Susanna

Comment

I work for a property company. One of my
colleagues is really lazy. When customers come
into the office, he tells me to note down all the
details. Then, if the client is looking for a very
expensive flat or house, he always takes them
to see the property. He never asks me to take
them. So his sales are much bigger than mine.
Last year, he got a much bigger bonus than me.
I wasn't happy about that. It's not fair because
I do all the hard work. Our boss really likes him.
She thinks he's a really good salesman.

Thomas

Comment

1 How can Susanna deal with the problem?

2 Do you agree with Thomas that 'it's not fair'?

🔊 **CD2.8** Listen to a voicemail from Matthew, who
called with a message for the magazine. What is his
problem? Note down the key points and summarise
the mistake that the Project Manager made.

Task

1 **Work in pairs. Discuss the problems
and decide what each person should
do to solve them.**

2 **Join another pair. Share information
about your decisions. Try to agree on
the right decision in each case.**

Writing

**You are reading the message board at
Office Life. Write a reply to one of the
people who left a message. Give your
reasons for the action you suggest.**

➡ *Writing file page 126*

UNIT 8 Advertising

'*Nobody counts the number of ads you run. They only remember the impression you make.*'
William Bernbach (1911–1982), US advertising executive

OVERVIEW

VOCABULARY
Advertising and markets

READING
TV commercials

language focus 1
Comparatives and superlatives

LISTENING
Good and bad advertising

LANGUAGE FOCUS 2
*much / a lot,
a little / a bit*

SKILLS
Participating in discussions

CASE STUDY
Excelsior Chocolate Products

STARTING UP **A** Do this advertising quiz. Compare your answers with a partner. Then turn to page 131 to check your answers.

1 The most common word in advertisements is:
a) *world.* b) *best.* c) *you.*

2 A short song used in advertising is called a:
a) jingle. b) pop-up. c) spot.

3 What do you call this? ✓
a) a slogan b) a logo c) a jingle

4 'Just do it', 'Always Coca-Cola' and 'Because I'm worth it' are all:
a) logos. b) jingles. c) slogans.

5 In what year did internet advertising begin?
a) 1990 b) 1994 c) 1998

6 Which company was the first to advertise on the Internet?
a) AT&T b) McDonald's c) Sony

7 How long is a typical TV commercial?
a) 20 seconds b) 30 seconds c) 40 seconds

8 Where do you find advertising billboards or hoardings?
a) on the Internet
b) in the street
c) on mobile phones

9 Dentsu, WPP, and Ogilvy and Mather are all advertising:
a) budgets. b) agencies. c) campaigns.

B What's your favourite advert? Why do you like it?

74

VOCABULARY
Advertising and markets

A   ◀)) CD2.9 **Listen and repeat these numbers.**

6,300	six thousand, three hundred
75,807	seventy-five thousand, eight hundred and seven
823,120	eight hundred and twenty-three thousand, one hundred and twenty
1,255,500	one million, two hundred and fifty-five thousand, five hundred
10.5%	ten point five per cent

B   ◀)) CD2.10 **Listen to part of a sales presentation and underline the correct number in each sentence.**

1   Last year, the company had a market share of _10.3_ / _103_ per cent.

2   Last year, for the launch of Sparkle Lite, the advertising budget increased by _30_ / _13_ per cent.

3   Last year, the company sold more than _850,000_ / _815,000_ units of Sparkle.

4   The new advertising campaign cost _€90,000_ / _€900,000_.

5   The company wants to increase its market share to _11.5_ / _11.9_ per cent.

6   Next year, the company wants to sell _210,000_ / _2,100,000_ units of Sparkle.

C   **Match the beginnings of the sentences (1–5) with their endings (a–e).**

1   Coca-Cola is a mass-market product; it

2   Selling special-interest holidays is a niche market; it

3   Rolex watches sell in a luxury market; they are

4   An export market

5   A home market

a)   is a small but often profitable market.

b)   is outside the producer's country.

c)   is in the producer's country.

d)   high-quality and expensive goods.

e)   sells to large numbers of people.

D   **In pairs, think of products which match the types of market in Exercise C.**

Nike shoes sell to a mass market.

Ferrari sports cars are a luxury-market product.

E   **Which medium is the best way to advertise these products (or the ones you discussed in Exercise D)? Choose from the list below. Discuss your ideas with a partner.**

> a smartphone   a perfume   a health magazine
> a sports car   a new chocolate bar

- newspapers/magazines (the press)
- online/internet ads
- billboards/hoardings
- TV/radio commercials
- mobile ads
- leaflets/flyers
- free samples

*See the **DVD-ROM** for the i-Glossary.*

READING
TV commercials

A **Before you read the article below, discuss these questions.**

1 Which four adjectives best describe a VW Beetle?

   big   fast   feminine   fun   masculine   powerful   safe   stylish   unusual

2 In your country, how popular is the Beetle? Who typically buys it?

B **As you read the article, think about these questions.**

1 How is the photo in the article related to the 2012 Beetle?

2 What kind of person did VW want to see the advert?

C **Choose the best option to complete these sentences.**

1 *An American / A German* agency created the commercial.

2 The 2012 Beetle has a more *masculine / feminine* design than the older New Beetle.

3 The target customer for the 2012 Beetle is *male / male and female* drivers.

4 The ad *shows / doesn't show* the new car in detail.

5 VW first showed the commercial on *US / German* TV.

6 VW first showed the car to the public at an event in *Shanghai / New York*.

D **In each box, match the words from the article to make word partnerships.**

1	advertising	a) break	4	create	d) male drivers/customers
2	commercial	b) event	5	launch	e) the 2012 Beetle
3	launch	c) agency	6	attract	f) a commercial

E **Work in pairs. Each choose a TV advertisement you like.**

1 Complete these sentences about the advertisement.

   It's an advertisement for …   *It shows …*

   The music for the ad is …   *I like the advertisement because …*

2 Tell another student about your advertisement.

FT

Volkswagen's Black Beetle ad
by Bernard Simon

In spring 2011, Volkswagen asked the US advertising agency Deutsch, LA to create a TV commercial to launch its latest car, the 2012 Beetle.
5   The 2012 Beetle is bigger, more powerful and more masculine in design than the earlier model, the New Beetle, launched in 1987. Head of Design Klaus Bischoff said, "We
10 wanted to give the car a stronger and more masculine look." The idea was to attract more male drivers. More women than men bought the New Beetle. (Sales to women were
15 61 per cent in 2010.) Luca De Meo, Marketing Director, wants to see a 50–50 split between men and women for the new car.

The 30-second advert shows a
20 beetle racing through a forest. The beetle has a racing stripe on its back and is much bigger than the other insects. It races past the other insects and cuts corners, just like a high-
25 performance car. At the end of the advertisement, the beetle changes into the outline of the car, in the shadows. The music for the advertisement is the rock song *Black*
30 *Betty*. Using an image of a beetle for the car is not the most original advertising idea, but the advert is fun to watch.

VW first showed the advert during
35 the commercial breaks of the American football Super Bowl in

April 2011. There is usually a lot of interest in the ads during these breaks, and companies can pay $3 million for
40 a 30-second commercial. Later that month, VW showed the new car to the public at launch events in three cities: first in Shanghai, then in Berlin and New York.

➡ page 152

LANGUAGE FOCUS 1
Comparatives and superlatives

- We compare two things with the comparative form of the adjective.
  *Sales of luxury cars were **higher** this year than last year.*
  *The Mercedes LX is **more expensive** than a Volkswagen.*
- We compare three or more things with the superlative form.
  *China is **our largest** market in Asia.*
  *What is **the most expensive** make of car?*

A 🔊 CD2.11 **Write the comparative forms of these adjectives. Then listen to check how they are pronounced.**

1 small ....
2 fast ....
3 slow ....
4 high ....
5 bad ....
6 good ....
7 competitive ....
8 efficient ....
9 interesting ....

B **Look at this chart. Decide whether the sentences below are true (T) or false (F). Correct the false ones.**

	VW Passat	Mazda MX-5	Mini Hatchback
Engine size	2.0 litre	1.8 litre	1.6 litre
Maximum speed	195 kph	195 kph	203 kph
Petrol consumption	4.6 litre / 100 km	7.3 litre / 100 km	5.4 litre / 100 km
Luggage compartment	566 litres	150 litres	160 litres
Length	4,769 mm	4,020 mm	3,699 mm
Price	€19,665	€19,174	€13,410

1 The Mazda is a faster car than the Mini.
2 The Mazda has a smaller luggage compartment than the Mini.
3 The Mini has better petrol consumption than the Passat.
4 The Mazda is more expensive than the Passat.
5 The Passat is more practical for a family than the Mini.

C **Complete these sentences about the cars in Exercise B. Use the comparative form of the adjectives in brackets.**

1 I think the Mazda is a *more stylish* car than the Mini. (*stylish*)
2 The Passat has a .... engine than the Mazda. (*powerful*)
3 Compared to the Passat, the Mini is .... to park in small spaces. (*easy*)
4 The Passat is .... to run .... the Mazda. (*cheap*)
5 The Passat is a .... car .... the Mini. (*spacious*)

D **Complete these conversations. Use the superlative form of the adjectives.**

1 A: Advertising on primetime TV is expensive.
   B: Yes, it's *the most expensive* time of the day to show an advert.
2 A: Nike's 'Write the future' commercial was very good.
   B: Yes, I think it was .... commercial in 2010.
3 A: 2009 was a bad year for the advertising industry.
   B: Yes, it was .... year I can remember.
4 A: China has a very high number of internet users.
   B: Yes, it has .... number of users in the world.

C   **Complete this article with the present simple or the present continuous form of the verbs in brackets.**

Profile PRET A MANGER

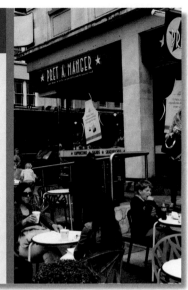

Pret A Manger ....._is_.....[1] (_be_) a UK company and one of the world's leading sandwich chains. It ....[2] (_sell_) freshly made sandwiches in busy city centres. At the end of each day, the shops ....[3] (_give_) any unsold products to the homeless. Currently, Pret ....[4] (_do_) very well in the south of England.

Pret ....[5] (_operate_) a total of 232 UK outlets, and this year it ....[6] (_plan_) new outlets for London. In the US, it ....[7] (_have_) 23 outlets in New York and another 10 in Hong Kong.

Pret's international activities ....[8] (_grow_) in importance. This month, as part of the next stage of expansion, Pret .... [9] (_open_) its first two shops in Paris. At the same time, the marketing team ....[10] (_work_) with Lewis PR, a global PR company, to improve the brand's international image.

D   **Work in pairs. Role-play this situation. Take it in turns to show each other around your company. Say what happens in each area and what is happening now.**

Student A

This is the main hall. We serve customers here. At the moment, a cashier is talking to a customer.

EBB Bank

Area	What happens	What is happening now
main hall	serve customers	cashier / talk / to a customer
currency section	exchange foreign currency	customer / change / dollars into euros
loans section	Assistant Manager arranges loans for customers	Assistant Manager / talk / to a customer on the phone
Manager's office	Manager works	Manager / meet / an important client
reception desk	staff answer questions from customers	receptionist / listen / to a customer's complaint

Student B

This is the kitchen. We prepare and cook meals here. At the moment, the chefs are preparing today's lunch.

Goldcrest Hotel

Area	What happens	What is happening now
kitchen	prepare and cook meals	chefs / prepare / today's lunch
restaurant	serve breakfast, lunch and dinner	waiter / clear / the tables
reception	welcome guests, answer calls	receptionist / talk / to a guest
gift shop	sell souvenirs	sales assistant / help / a customer
a bedroom	guests stay	maid / clean / the room

SKILLS

Starting a presentation

Watch the presentation on the DVD-ROM.

A 🔊 CD2.20 **Listen to the start of a presentation. Number these items (a–f) in the order you hear them.**

a) There are three parts to my presentation. Firstly, … ☐

b) By the end of my presentation, you will understand clearly our future plans. ☐

c) Good afternoon, everyone. My name's Robert Ford. ☐ 1

d) If you don't mind, let's leave questions to the end. ☐

e) I'd like to talk about our new marketing strategy. ☐

f) Finally, the details of the costs … ☐

B 🔊 CD2.20 **Listen again. Match the headings (1–5) to the items (a–f) in Exercise A. One heading goes with two items.**

1 Topic of the talk

2 Aim

3 Greeting the audience

4 Plan of the talk

5 Dealing with questions

C **Work in pairs. Prepare an introduction to a presentation. Then introduce the presentation to each other. Choose Role A or Role B below, and use the notes to introduce your presentation. Add any information you wish.**

Role A	Role B
Topic The launch of your company's new product	**Topic** Your company's new teleconferencing system
Plan 1 The background to the launch 2 The features of the new product 3 The advertising and marketing plans	**Plan** 1 The background – why we need to change 2 The new system and its benefits 3 How to use it and to report faults
Aim To give a clear idea of the sales potential of the product	**Aim** To give a clear idea of how the new teleconferencing system improves communication in the company

USEFUL LANGUAGE

GREETING

Good morning/afternoon. I'm …

Hello, everyone. Nice to see you again.

Hi, I'm …. Good to see you all.

TOPIC

My subject today is our new product launch.

I'd like to talk to you about the bonus scheme.

I'm going to talk about our sales strategy.

The subject of my presentation is overseas expansion.

PLAN OF THE TALK

There are three parts to my presentation.

My presentation is in three sections.

Firstly, …

Secondly, …

Finally, …

AIMS

By the end of my presentation, you will have a clear idea of the new system.

By the end of my talk, you will understand how/why this benefits us all.

At the end of the presentation, you will know more about the direction we plan to take.

Presenting your company

How to make a good impression

Background

You are beginning a training course on giving presentations. The trainer has provided a structure for an introduction (see below). She asks you to introduce yourself and the company you work for. You are all from different parts of the world and different industries.

🔊 **CD2.21** At the beginning of the course, the trainer gives a model presentation. Listen, then answer these questions.

1. What is the aim of the presentation?
2. Where is Fiestatime's most important store?
3. What are its turnover and profit?
4. What does the company plan to do next year?

Structure for presentation

A Greeting
- Your name
- Your position

B Topic
- Subject/purpose of talk

C Plan of talk
- Sections/parts of talk

D Facts and figures
- Company products or services
- Important figures: number of employees, turnover, profits
- Your main competitors
- Your duties

E Future developments
- Your plans for next year

Task

1. Work in small groups. Read your company profile.

   Student A: Turn to page 133.
   Student B: Turn to page 142.
   Student C: Turn to page 143.

2. Prepare a short presentation about yourself and the company you work for. It should last approximately one minute.

3. Make your presentation to the other members of your group. Try to answer any questions they ask.

4. As a group, decide what you liked about each presentation. Why was it interesting?

Writing

You are a representative of your company. Write a short profile of the company for the company website. Include some of the information from your presentation.

➡ *Writing file* page 129

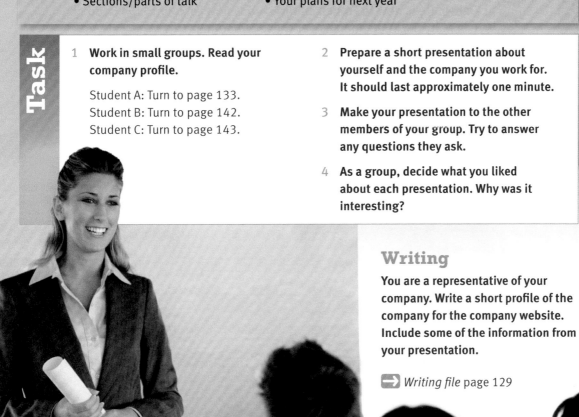

Case study

3 Doing business internationally

A A meeting in France

What do you know about business in France? In pairs, decide whether these statements are true (T) or false (F).

1 It is common for people to work for lots of different companies in their career.

2 Business lunches are usually very short and focus on work.

3 People's educational background is very important.

4 Most major French companies have their headquarters in Paris.

5 Appointments are not usually necessary and are often made just a day in advance.

6 July and August is a common holiday period and not the best time for arranging meetings.

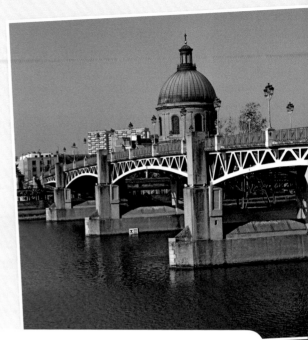

Task 1

1 ◀)) CD2.22 Ryan Miller is a salesman for a medical equipment distributor in the south of France. He is new to French culture and is now talking to the Head of Sales, Sylvie Martin. Listen and answer these questions.

1 Where was the business meeting?
2 When was the business meeting?
3 Where were the headquarters?
4 Did Ryan go to a university?

2 ◀)) CD2.22 Listen again and discuss what Ryan did not understand about French culture. Use the answers from Exercise A to help you. If necessary, look at the audio script on page 165.

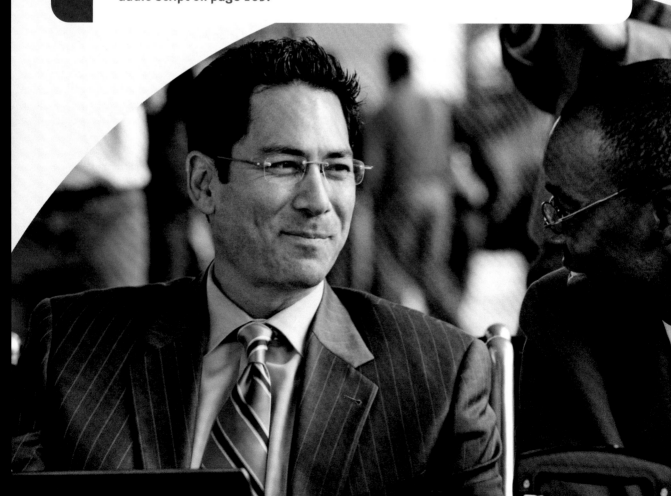

B Doing business in Russia

Task 2

1 ◄)) CD2.23–2.25 **Listen to three people talking about their business trips to Russia on a business radio programme and answer these questions.**

1 Which cities did the people visit?

2 Which speaker had the most successful business trip?

3 Which speaker had the least successful business trip?

2 ◄)) CD2.23–2.25 **Listen again and take notes about the key points in each extract.**

3 **Write a list of tips for someone going on a business trip to Russia.**

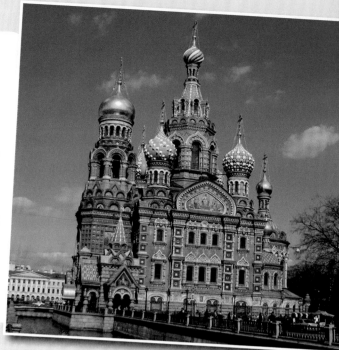

C In a Colombian home

Susan Forbes is a cultural-awareness consultant specialising in Latin America. She is running a workshop on doing business in Colombia. She talks about her first business trip to Bogotá, when she was invited to a Colombian home. Before you listen, read these tips for doing business in Colombia.

1 For social occasions, it is normal to arrive 30 minutes after the invitation time.

2 When invited to a home for a meal, bring flowers, chocolates, nuts or fruit. Wrapped gifts are opened in private. Do not mention the gifts again.

3 Always allow the host to make the first toast.

4 Good topics for conversation are culture, soccer, history, literature and coffee.

5 It is rude not to accept a cup of coffee at someone's home.

Task 3

1 ◄)) CD2.26 **Listen to Susan Forbes talking about her first business trip. Take notes on what she did well and what mistakes she made. The tips above will help you.**

2 **In groups, discuss what Susan did well and what mistakes she made.**

D Work in groups. Think about the business cultures of the three countries in this section: France, Russia and Colombia.

1 Which of these countries would you like to visit? Discuss your answers with other members of your group and give reasons.

2 Choose one of the three countries. How does your own business culture differ from the country you have chosen? In what ways is it similar?

7 People

VOCABULARY

Read these two descriptions, then tick (✓) the words below that best describe each person.

> Ahmed Adib spends a lot of time on his work and he does a very good job. He also has a lot of new ideas. He likes to be on time for work and for meetings, but he's also usually very calm. He works very well, and he encourages other people to work well.

> Elizabet Martens always does what she promises to do. This is probably because she wants to reach the top in her career. She's very good at making things work, and she likes to do things for other people. In fact, she really likes to spend time with other people, and other people like to spend time with her.

	Ahmed Adib	Elizabet Martens
ambitious	☐	☐
creative	☐	☐
hard-working	☐	☐
helpful	☐	☐
motivating	☐	☐
practical	☐	☐
punctual	☐	☐
relaxed	☐	☐
reliable	☐	☐
sociable	☐	☐

PAST SIMPLE: NEGATIVES AND QUESTIONS

Complete these sentences with *was, wasn't, were, weren't, did* or *didn't*.

1 Benoît .... born in France, he was born in Switzerland.

2 We .... play golf at the weekend because the weather was terrible.

3 .... you see Alfredo yesterday?

4 Elena and Piet .... in the office last week because they were at a conference in Tokyo.

5 How .... your holiday?

6 A: I saw Mikhail and Jenna at the conference yesterday.

   B: .... they well?

7 .... the presentation good?

8 I .... meet Helena because she wasn't in the office.

9 The underground trains .... running yesterday because there was a strike.

10 A: I visited the Hamburg office last week.

   B: Oh, good. .... you see Karl?

SKILLS

Complete the conversation below using the words from the box.

'll   'm   's   do   don't   have   is   look   need   think

A: I ....[1] some training in accounting to ....[2] my job properly.

B: I ....[3] sorry. It's just not possible.

A: It ....[4] really important for me.

B: The problem ....[5], we don't ....[6] the money for this. Why ....[7] you buy a self-study course?

A: OK, I ....[8] take a look at one.

B: I think you should ....[9] for one at an online bookshop.

A: OK, I'll ....[10] about it.

8 Advertising

VOCABULARY

Complete the missing numbers.

1	....	four thousand, five hundred
2	36,589	....
3	....	eight hundred and thirty-nine thousand, two hundred and thirty
4	1,433,900	....
5	....	fourteen point six per cent
6	2,870	....
7	....	fifty-six thousand, eight hundred and one
8	217,418	....
9	....	five million, two hundred and eighty-four thousand, five hundred and sixty-six
10	98.3%	....

COMPARATIVES AND SUPERLATIVES

Look at these sales figures for three electronics retailers. Then complete the article below with the correct words and phrases from the box.

	Sales €m	% change
Teevee Land (38 shops)	27	+7
Planet Electronica (22 shops)	15	+15
EGS (10 shops)	16	+19

a little   fewest   lower   more interesting   much   the most   the most impressive

The three most popular electronics retailers performed well last year. If we look at the sales figures, we can see that Teevee Land's sales were ....[1] higher that its competitors', while Planet Electronica's sales were just ....[2] lower than EGS's. But the percentage change in sales is ....[3] than the sales figures. Teevee Land, the company with ....[4] shops, shows much ....[5] growth than its competitors. It is, in fact, EGS, the company with the ....[6] shops, which has ....[7] growth in sales.

Use the information in this table to write a short report (about 100 words) comparing the two shampoos.

	Bottle size	Selling price	Target market	Main outlet	Sales	% change (year-on-year sales)
HairGlow	250ml	€14	18–25	hairdressers	1st quarter €141,500 2nd quarter €232,000	+9
Sheen	300ml	€10	26–50	supermarkets	1st quarter €202,500 2nd quarter €195,000	+11

9 Companies

Complete the text below using the words from the box.

ITS Electronics ....¹ electronic components. The company ....² the home electronics industry – companies that............³ TVs, stereos and so on. Isomu Takahashi ....⁴ ITS in 1989. The company ....⁵ about 90 people and............⁶ to about 10 countries. ITS does its own research and development and............⁷ six or eight new products each year.

employs   exports   introduces   manufactures   produce   started   supplies

Complete this text with the best form of the verbs in brackets: present simple or present continuous.

My company............¹ (*manufacture*) and............² (*export*) frozen fish products. We ....³ (*buy*) our fish directly from local fishermen. Right now, we............⁴ (*make*) plans to increase our production. So we............⁵ (*need*) to find different suppliers for fish. Our main customers............⁶ (*be*) restaurant chains abroad. However, right now, we............⁷ (*plan*) a new range of frozen meals because we............⁸ (*want*) to enter the consumer market. So at the moment, our marketing team............⁹ (*do*) a lot of research. They............¹⁰ (*try*) to understand our target market.

Complete this introduction to a presentation with the correct prepositions.

Hi, I'm Elena Martinez. Good to see you all. I'd like to talk............¹ you............²
the new computer network. My presentation is............³ three sections. The subject
............⁴ the first part............⁵ my presentation is the installation schedule. After
that, I'm going to talk............⁶ the benefits of the new software. Finally, I'll explain the
training programme. By the end............⁷ my presentation, you will have a clear idea
............⁸ the new network.

Blakelock Engineering

A company has some bad news to communicate

Background

Blakelock Engineering is losing money. To cut costs and improve profits, it is going to reduce its employees by 100. This represents about 10 per cent of the workforce. There are two important decisions to make:

1   who will leave the company;

2   how to communicate with two groups: the staff and the company's shareholders.

🔊 **CD2.36.** Listen to a company director talking to the Head of Human Resources. Note down the three ways they could use to decide who leaves the company. Are there any other ways they could consider?

Arrangements for a meeting

Helen Dawson joined Blakelock six months ago. She works in the design department. Like many staff, she is very worried about losing her job. She calls the Head of Human Resources to arrange a meeting with him. She wants to find out if the company will ask her to leave. The Head of Human Resources does not want to meet her at this time. The management has not yet decided who will have to leave the company. He makes excuses for not meeting her.

Work in pairs. Role-play their conversation.

Task

Work in pairs. You are directors of the company.

1   Discuss the various ways of choosing who will leave the company. What are the advantages and disadvantages of each way? Which way is the best?

2   Decide on the best way to communicate your decision to a) the staff, and b) the shareholders. Say who should communicate your decision.

3   Compare your solutions with another pair.

4   Work as one group. Discuss how the company can help the employees who will be leaving Blakelock Engineering.

Writing

You are the Managing Director of Blakelock Engineering. Write an e-mail to all the staff, announcing a meeting to discuss the present situation of the company. Give the date, time and place of the meeting. Mention that all the directors will attend. Say that you will talk about the company's plans for improving profits.

➡ *Writing file page 126*

OVERVIEW

VOCABULARY
Company cultures

LISTENING
Cultural mistakes

LANGUAGE FOCUS 1
should/shouldn't

READING
Cultural differences

LANGUAGE FOCUS 2
could/would

SKILLS
Identifying problems and agreeing action

CASE STUDY
The wind of change

STARTING UP

A **Imagine you are visiting a country for the first time to do business. Complete the tips below using the words from the box on the left.**

> cards   clothes   date
> customs   food   gifts
> hours   language
> leaders   money
> ~~sport~~

1   Find out about the most popular *sport* in the country.

2   Always take .... in US dollars.

3   Find out about the normal working ....

4   Be careful how you write the ....

5   Find out about the most important .... and festivals.

6   Learn to speak a little of the local ....

7   Try some of the .... before you go.

8   Wear formal ....

9   Translate your business .... into the local language.

10 Take some .... for your hosts which are typical of your own country.

11 Learn something about the most famous business .... and celebrities.

B **Which of the tips in Exercise A do you think are: a) very useful? b) useful? c) not useful?**

Why? Compare your ideas with a partner.

C **Add some other tips for visitors to your country.**

VOCABULARY

Company cultures

A Different companies have different cultures and ways of working. Complete these sentences with the items in brackets. One of the items in each section cannot be used.

Dress (uniforms / ~~casual Fridays~~ / weekend clothes)

1 We don't have to wear business suits at the end of the week. My company has a system of *casual Fridays.*

2 In many banks, staff can't wear what they like. They have to wear ....

Timekeeping (flexitime / part-time / shift work)

3 For two weeks each month, I work at night. I can't sleep during the day. I hate ....

4 We have a .... system in our office. Some people choose to work from 9 a.m. to 5 p.m.; others work from 10 a.m. to 6 p.m.

Time off (childcare / annual leave / public holiday)

5 I am so busy at the moment that I worked on New Year's Day, which is a(n) ....

6 How many days' .... do you get in your company?

Reporting procedures (written report / face to face / e-mail)

7 We often speak on the phone, but never ....

8 He uploads a(n) .... on the company intranet each month.

Types of meeting (informal / formal / social)

9 Our department starts every day with a(n) .... meeting. It is very relaxed.

10 Companies have an Annual General Meeting (AGM) once a year. It is a very .... meeting, with a lot of people.

Names (job title / first name / family names)

11 In some countries, the company culture is formal. Staff use .... when they speak to each other.

12 What's your .... now? Are you Chief Executive?

B Would you like to work for an organisation which has:

• uniforms?   • a lot of formal meetings?   • casual Fridays?   • flexible hours?

C Match each phrase (1–5) to its explanation (a–e).

A positive company culture ...

1 empowers employees.

2 supports innovation.

3 is customer focused.

4 rewards good performance.

5 encourages trust at all levels.

a) New ideas and change are welcome.

b) Relationships between employees and managers are open and honest.

c) Staff have a lot of control over their work.

d) The needs and wants of the customers always come first.

e) There is an incentive scheme for efficient employees.

D Work in pairs. Put the five characteristics in Exercise C in order of importance for you, and explain why.

*See the **DVD-ROM** for the i-Glossary.*

E What are the beliefs and values of your organisation? Discuss in groups.

LISTENING
Cultural mistakes

Three people talk about cultural mistakes.

A ◀))) CD2.37 **Listen to John's story and answer these questions.**

1 What meal was John invited to? *dinner*
2 What did he look at?
3 What was his mistake?

    a) He talked during an important silence.

    b) He talked about his host's table.

    c) He didn't want a gift.

B ◀))) CD2.38 **Listen to Cameron's story and answer these questions.**

1 Where was Peter's new job?
2 What was his mistake?

    a) He did not use first names.

    b) He did not speak French.

    c) He did not use family names.

3 How did the staff feel when Peter used first names?

C ◀))) CD2.39 **Listen to Susan's story and answer these questions.**

1 Where did Susan make her mistake?
2 Who did she go out for a meal with?
3 What was her mistake?

    a) She poured her own drink.

    b) She did not laugh.

    c) She poured too many drinks.

4 What did she forget to do?

D ◀))) CD2.40–2.42 **Listen to Liz, Jeremy and Ros talking about cultural mistakes.**

Which speaker ...	Liz	Jeremy	Ros
1 was working in East Africa?			
2 was working with a Dutch colleague?	✓		
3 got straight down to business?			
4 writes long e-mails?			
5 often adds funny comments in e-mails?			
6 thought a colleague was abrupt and rude?			

Watch the interviews on the DVD-ROM.

Liz Credé

Jeremy Keeley

Ros Pomeroy

E **It is easy to make mistakes in other cultures. What other examples do you know?**

LANGUAGE FOCUS 1

should/
shouldn't

- We use *should* and *shouldn't* to give advice and make suggestions.
  We **should** wear formal clothes to the dinner.
  You **shouldn't** be late for meetings.

- We often use *I think* or *I don't think* with *should* to say something is or isn't a good idea.
  I think you **should** go on a training course.
  I don't think you **should** interrupt her.
  '**Do you think** I **should** learn to speak the local language?' 'Yes, **I do**. / No, **I don't**.'

➡ page 155

A **Complete the sentences below using *should* or *shouldn't* and a phrase from the box.**

| speak to our boss   buy an expensive computer system |
| be late   ~~develop a better website~~   stay three days |

1 Our online business is bad.

   We ..... *should develop a better website* ..... .

2 Our team is working too many hours.

   We ....

3 The meeting is very important.

   We ....

4 She wants to visit a lot of customers in Spain.

   She ....

5 We have to control our costs.

   You ....

B **Give the opposite advice by using *should*, *shouldn't* or *I don't think*.**

1 I think he should get a salary increase.

   I don't think he should get a salary increase.

2 I think we should launch the new product now.

3 She shouldn't take customers to expensive restaurants.

4 We should take every customer complaint seriously.

5 I think staff should fly economy on every trip.

C **Work in pairs. Your colleague is going on a business trip. Take turns to ask for and give advice using the notes below.**

A: *I'm going on a business trip. Do you have any advice?*

B: *You shouldn't stay in an expensive hotel.*

- Stay in an expensive hotel. ✗

- Take plenty of business cards. ✓

- Arrange a lot of appointments on the same day. ✗

- Be late for appointments. ✗

- Write a short report after each meeting. ✓

- Keep all your receipts for travel and restaurants. ✓

Cultural differences

A Do you agree with these statements?

1 All meetings should have fixed start and finishing times.

2 Being on time is equally important in all situations.

3 It's more important to learn about the culture of the country you do business with than to learn the language.

4 There's no point having a detailed plan before you start a project. Things always change, and you need to be very flexible.

B As you read the article below, think about this question.

What are two main causes of cultural misunderstanding between Brazil and China?

FT

Lessons in cultural difference

by Samantha Pearson

1 It is 9.05 a.m. and a group of Chinese businessmen are outside a hotel conference room in São Paulo, waiting for their Brazilian hosts. The seminar was scheduled to start five minutes ago, but, like many meetings in Brazil, it did not start on time. The Brazilians arrive, complaining loudly about the morning's traffic and go immediately to breakfast. Cultural differences between the two countries become clear.

2 In 2009, China replaced the US as Brazil's biggest trading partner.

As a result, Brazilian companies are keen to understand the Chinese better and find the best way to do business together.

3 For companies already working with China, getting to know the culture is a priority. At Chinbra, São Paulo's biggest Chinese language school, students, who mainly work in the import business, take evening classes in Mandarin. About half the lesson is about cultural issues. They ask questions such as "Should I give my business card with two hands?" and "What presents should I give – something Brazilian?".

4 Some business deals fail because of small things like a misunderstood e-mail. "In addition to language problems, there is also a lack of cultural understanding between the two countries," says Charles Tang, president of the Brazil–China Chamber of Commerce.

5 One big issue is timing. For

successful deals with the Chinese, it is important to be on time for meetings and to meet deadlines. Another issue is planning. In Brazil, because of high inflation during the 1980s and early 1990s and many failed plans, long-term planning was not a priority. Today, many companies still prefer to plan as they go along and fix problems when they happen. The Chinese are completely different. They like to plan everything in advance and in detail.

C Decide whether these statements about the article are true (T) or false (F). Correct the false ones.

1 Brazil's biggest trading partner today is the US. *F (It's now China.)*

2 At Chinbra, students spend most of the time learning Mandarin.

3 Charles Tang thinks deals go wrong mainly because of language problems.

4 For the Chinese, being on time is very important.

5 Brazilians don't give a lot of importance to planning.

D Work in pairs. Read the situation at the beginning of the article again (paragraph 1) and discuss these questions.

1 What happened?

2 How do you think both sides felt about the situation?

3 For the next meeting with the Chinese, what could the Brazilians do differently?

E **Find words in the article with these meanings.**

1 planned (paragraph 1) *scheduled*

2 very important and needing attention (paragraph 3)

3 problems (paragraph 3)

4 to be unsuccessful (paragraph 4)

5 when there is not enough of something (paragraph 4)

6 the last possible date for doing something (paragraph 5)

F **Work in pairs. What practical advice would you give about studying or doing business in your country? Discuss two or three of these points.**

- appointments
- meetings/seminars
- giving gifts
- greetings
- planning and deadlines
- making friends

LANGUAGE FOCUS 2
could/would

- We often use *could* to make a polite request.
  Could I use your mobile phone, please?
  Could you send me a copy of the report, please?

- We often use *would you like* to make an offer.
  Would you like a brochure?

➡ page 155

A **These questions were asked on a plane journey. Decide whether they were asked by the flight attendant (F) or the passenger (P).**

1 Could I have another drink, please?

2 Would you like a newspaper?

3 Could you show me how to turn on the light, please?

4 Would you like another drink?

5 Could I have some mineral water, please?

6 Would you like coffee or tea?

7 Could you fasten your seat belt, please?

8 Could you help me find the movie channel, please?

B **Which of the questions in Exercise A are offers, and which are requests?**

C **You are at a hotel reception desk. Use the verbs in brackets to make polite requests.**

1 You need a map of the city. (*have*) *Could I have a map of the city, please?*

2 You want to go to a good restaurant. (*recommend*)

3 You didn't hear that. (*say*)

4 You want a photocopy of a document. (*copy*)

5 You want your bill. (*have*)

6 You want a taxi. (*call*)

D ◀)) CD2.43 **Listen to the requests in Exercise C to check.**

E ◀)) CD2.43 **Listen again. How does the other person reply?**

F Work in pairs. You are organising a visit to your company's factory. Take turns to make and reply to the requests on page 133.

A: *Could I have last month's production figures?*

B: *Yes, I'll e-mail them to you this afternoon.*

SKILLS

Identifying problems and agreeing action

A ◀)) CD2.44 Louise, a project manager, is in a meeting with Tom, one of the project team leaders. They are talking about Paul, a foreign consultant hired by head office to work on the project. Listen to the conversation. Decide whether these statements are true (T) or false (F). Correct the false ones.

1 Tom does not have a good relationship with Paul.

2 Tom would like Paul to communicate more face to face.

3 Paul gets on well with the customers because of his knowledge.

4 Paul does not meet his colleagues very often after work.

5 Louise is going to have a meeting with all the team members first.

B CD2.44 Listen again and complete these extracts.

L: What ....¹ is the problem?

T: You see, Paul's not very good at ....².

T: Well, how can I put it? They respect him, he's got a lot of ....³.

L: Well, I think the ....⁴ thing to do is for me to have a talk with him. I'll give him some good ....⁵.

*Watch the meeting on the **DVD-ROM**.*

C Work in pairs. Look at the audio script on page 166. Imagine you are the project manager. What advice are you going to give Paul? Make a list of three points.

D Complete these sentences (1–4) with suitable endings (a–d).

1 The problem is,

2 I think you should

3 The best thing to do

4 OK. So you're going

a) to have a meeting with him first.

b) he's not good at communicating.

c) talk to him first.

d) is to explain what his role is.

E Role-play this situation. Two managers in the same department have a problem with an employee, Ken Darby. They meet to discuss what to do.

Student A: Turn to page 137.

Student B: Turn to page 142.

USEFUL LANGUAGE

OPENING

There's something I'd like to talk to you about.

I need to talk to you about something.

Could I have a word with you?

STATING THE TOPIC

There's a problem with Paul.

The problem is, we don't have a good relationship.

SUGGESTING ACTION

We could meet the other members of the team.

I think / don't think we should meet Paul every week.

One thing we could do is talk to him.

We should/shouldn't move him to another department.

The best thing to do is explain his role to the team.

RESPONDING TO SUGGESTIONS

I agree. We'll meet him as soon as possible.

Fine. Let's talk to him.

Yes. I think that would be very helpful.

I'm not sure that's a good idea.

Well, I'm not sure about that.

Mmm. I don't think that's a good idea.

The wind of change

A manager wants to bring in new ideas and change the company culture

Background

Kate Maskie is the new General Manager in an overseas branch of Far Eastern Traders, an international clothing company. She wants to bring the best new ideas from head office to the overseas branch.

Kate wants:	Overseas branch culture now
all staff to use first names.	Staff use family names.
all staff to dress casually at work.	Staff dress formally at all times.
to introduce a system of flexible working hours.	Working hours are fixed (9.00 a.m. to 5.00 p.m.).
to keep all meetings to 30 minutes only.	There are many long, formal meetings.
to introduce hot-desking* to the open-plan office.	Most staff have their own space in the open-plan office.
an 'open-door' policy, so staff can see a manager at any time.	Staff need an appointment to see any manager.

* 'Hot-desking' is a system where you do not have your own desk in the office, but use any desk that is free.

◄)) **CD2.45** Listen to Kate Maskie as she talks to Stuart Adams, her manager at head office, about the problems. Discuss these questions.

1 Why does Kate want to change the culture in the branch office?

2 What problem will she face?

3 What will Kate do at the meeting?

Task

Kate and Stuart meet some of the senior staff to discuss the ideas for a new company culture.

1 Work in groups of four and choose a role.

Kate Maskie: Turn to page 139.
Director of Human Resources: Turn to page 141.

Stuart Adams: Turn to page 140.
Finance Director: Turn to page 144.

2 Look at your role cards and prepare for the meeting.

3 Meet and discuss Kate's ideas. Decide what you will change and what you will keep the same.

Writing

Write the action minutes of the meeting.

FAR EASTERN TRADERS

Subject: New ideas from head office   Date:

Participants:

Agenda item		Decision	Reason	Action	Name
1	Staff to use first names				
2	Staff to dress casually on Fridays only				

➡ *Writing file page 128*

UNIT 12 Jobs

'All jobs are easy to the person who doesn't have to do them.'
Holt's Law

STARTING UP

A Look at these jobs. Who do you think should get the highest salary? Put the jobs in order, highest salary first.

- lawyer
- nurse
- professional footballer
- accountant
- fashion model

- postal worker
- firefighter
- teacher
- advertising executive
- air-traffic controller

- doctor
- banker
- architect
- sales assistant
- farmer

B Which jobs have the highest/lowest salaries in your country? Compare your ideas with a partner.

C Which of the following would you like (✓) or not like (✗) in a job?

1 a lot of telephone work
2 writing lots of reports
3 working with the same people
4 working with a lot of different people
5 working on your own
6 working flexible hours (including weekends)

7 using English at work
8 sharing an office
9 casual dress
10 a lot of targets and deadlines
11 travelling to other countries
12 a uniform

D Which is more important to you, a high salary or a job you enjoy? Why?

A Complete the first part of the advertisement below with the verbs from the box. Use the words in brackets to help you.

| cope with | develop | improve | increase | ~~lead~~ | set up | train |

KARADA MODE PLC
EUROPEAN MANAGER €95K + CAR

Are you the person we are looking for?

THE ROLE

We are looking for a talented person for this position. In this exciting job, you will need to:

- ..lead..[1] a team of 25. (*be in charge of*)
- ....[2] a new branch in Amsterdam. (*start*)
- ....[3] new staff. (*teach*)
- ....[4] sales in all markets. (*make more*)
- ....[5] new products. (*create*)
- ....[6] communication between our head office and local branches. (*make better*)
- ....[7] strict deadlines and work well under pressure. (*manage*)

B Complete the second part of the advertisement with the verbs from the box.

| deal with | manage | motivate | organise | plan |

THE PERSON

In your present job, you:

- ....[1] a large department in the clothing industry. (*control*)
- ....[2] budgets. (*think about the future*)
- ....[3] sales conferences and trade exhibitions. (*arrange*)
- ....[4] customers, suppliers and their problems. (*take action*)
- ....[5] employees and sales teams to get the best results. (*encourage*)

C Describe your role in your present or a past job. Use the verbs from Exercises A and B.

*See the **DVD-ROM** for the i-Glossary.*

In my present job, I lead a team of three.

In my last job, I trained staff to use the new IT system.

LANGUAGE FOCUS 1

Present perfect

- We use the present perfect to talk about situations that began in the past and continue in the present.
  *I **have worked** for IBM for five years.* (And I'm still working here now.)
  *They **have lived** in Barcelona for two years.* (And they are still living there now.)

- We often use the present perfect to talk about life experiences.
  *I **have had** three jobs since I left university.*
  *She **hasn't had** any experience in marketing.*
  *'**Have** you ever **worked** abroad?' 'Yes, I **have**.' / 'No, I **haven't**.'*

- The present perfect is formed with *have/has* + the past participle of the main verb.

➡ page 156

A Complete these sentences with the present perfect form of the verbs in brackets.

1 I *have given* (*give*) two presentations this month.

2 I .... (*not send*) any e-mails today.

3 He .... (*change*) jobs recently.

4 Magda .... (*be*) away on business all week.

5 They .... (*not have*) any experience in negotiating.

B Match the job interview questions (1–5) to their answers (a–e).

1 How many jobs have you had since leaving university?

2 Why have you changed jobs so often?

3 What have you done that shows leadership?

4 In what ways has your job changed since you joined the company?

5 Have you ever worked with a difficult person?

a) I now have more responsibility and I plan the sales strategy for the team.

b) Well, I lead the sales team. I'm also chairperson of a local business association.

c) I wanted to get experience of sales in different industries.

d) Well, the boss in my last company wasn't very easy to work with.

e) I've worked for six companies.

C 🔊 CD2.46 **Now listen and check your answers.**

D Complete these interview questions using the present perfect form of the verbs in brackets.

1 How *have you changed* (*you change*) over the last five years?

2 What software programs .... (*you use*) recently?

3 What .... (*you learn*) from your other jobs?

4 What sort of problems .... (*you have*) to deal with?

5 What part of your job .... (*you enjoy*) the most?

6 Which countries .... (*you visit*) for work/study?

E **Work in pairs. Ask and answer the questions in Exercise D.**

LISTENING
My ideal job

Liz Credé

A 🔊 CD2.47 Listen to the first part of an interview with Liz Credé, an organisation development consultant. In pairs, take notes on what she says about:

1 her current job

2 a job she had over 20 years ago.

Then compare your notes with your partner's.

B 🔊 CD2.48 **Listen to the second part of the interview and decide whether these statements are true (T) or false (F). Correct the false ones.**

1 Her strengths come from her work as a CEO over the last 20 years.

2 She understands how organisations work by studying them closely.

3 She can see a situation from many different sides.

4 She finds it easy to make decisions.

C 🔊 CD2.49 **Listen to the final part of the interview. Complete these notes on the advice that Liz gives.**

- Take the ....[1] that you are given and ....[2] as much as you can from them.
- Really ....[3] to those around you and pay ....[4] to what they are saying.
- Build ....[5] across the organisation.
- Ask a question that demonstrates you're really ....[6] in the company.

Watch the interview on the DVD-ROM.

D **In pairs, discuss these questions.**

1 What are your strengths and weaknesses?

2 What kinds of people do you work well with?

3 What is your ideal job?

READING
Professional networking sites

A **Ask and answer these questions in small groups.**

1 Do you have a profile on a professional networking website such as LinkedIn? If so, which one? How do you use it?

2 Does your company/university have a profile on a professional networking website? If so, which one?

3 Discuss how a professional networking site can help individuals and companies / educational institutions.

It can be useful for finding a job / getting new business.

B **Look at Helen Braoudakis's profile on a professional networking site on page 116. Put these headings in the correct place on the profile.**

~~Recruitment professional~~   Education   Specialities
Interests   Work experience   Professional summary

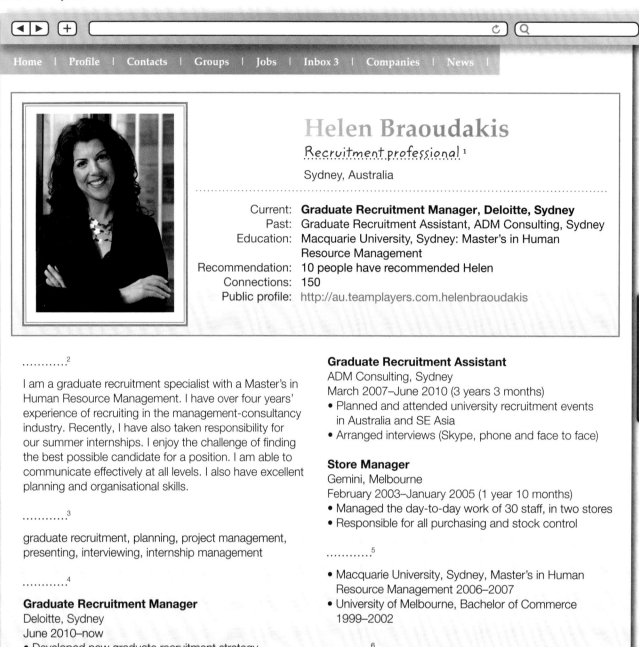

Profile page:

Home | Profile | Contacts | Groups | Jobs | Inbox 3 | Companies | News |

Helen Braoudakis
Recruitment professional [1]

Sydney, Australia

Current: **Graduate Recruitment Manager, Deloitte, Sydney**
Past: Graduate Recruitment Assistant, ADM Consulting, Sydney
Education: Macquarie University, Sydney: Master's in Human Resource Management
Recommendation: 10 people have recommended Helen
Connections: 150
Public profile: http://au.teamplayers.com.helenbraoudakis

..........[2]

I am a graduate recruitment specialist with a Master's in Human Resource Management. I have over four years' experience of recruiting in the management-consultancy industry. Recently, I have also taken responsibility for our summer internships. I enjoy the challenge of finding the best possible candidate for a position. I am able to communicate effectively at all levels. I also have excellent planning and organisational skills.

..........[3]

graduate recruitment, planning, project management, presenting, interviewing, internship management

..........[4]

Graduate Recruitment Manager
Deloitte, Sydney
June 2010–now
• Developed new graduate recruitment strategy.
• Set up and ran summer internship programme for 60 candidates

Graduate Recruitment Assistant
ADM Consulting, Sydney
March 2007–June 2010 (3 years 3 months)
• Planned and attended university recruitment events in Australia and SE Asia
• Arranged interviews (Skype, phone and face to face)

Store Manager
Gemini, Melbourne
February 2003–January 2005 (1 year 10 months)
• Managed the day-to-day work of 30 staff, in two stores
• Responsible for all purchasing and stock control

..........[5]

• Macquarie University, Sydney, Master's in Human Resource Management 2006–2007
• University of Melbourne, Bachelor of Commerce 1999–2002

..........[6]

other cultures, teaching scuba diving, playing the guitar, cooking

C Decide whether these statements are true (T) or false (F). Correct the false ones.

1 Helen did her Master's in HRM in Melbourne.

2 She has worked for three different companies.

3 She has always worked in graduate recruitment.

4 She has good communication skills.

5 When she was at ADM Consulting, she was responsible for organising summer internships.

6 She doesn't have any experience outside Australia.

D Write a summary for a professional networking profile. Use the example summary above. Include information about your experience, qualifications, skills and personal qualities.

Weaknesses:

5 Well, to be ...., I've always .... to work alone.

6 The courses have been very ....

7 I know I'll .... this in future.

3 🔊 BSA4.1.19 **Listen to the telephone call Adam gets a week later. Did he get the job?**

E SPEAKING 2

Work in pairs. Practise answering some common interview questions. Give feedback.

Student A: Turn to page x.

Student B: Turn to page vii.

Task

Pre-task: Research

1 You have applied for the job below and you received an e-mail response this morning. Read the job description and the e-mail and take notes.

INTERNATIONAL BUSINESS REPORTERS

Home based, $50 per hour, 5 hours per week, Business Online

We are a popular international website and we are recruiting people with business knowledge to write short, weekly reports on business news and activities for our international audience. Candidates must speak English, be organised and must be able to communicate ideas to others clearly.

2 weeks ago

Dear Mr / Mrs .... ,

Thank you for your interest in *Business Online*.
We have looked at your application and we would like to talk further. Are you able to attend an online interview next Monday, at 4 o'clock?

We look forward to speaking to you.

Rita Chopra,

Content Editor

2 Write a short reply to Rita Chopra, accepting the invitation. Use the e-mail in Exercise C to help you.

Part 1: Preparation

1 Work in pairs or small groups. Read the context.

Context: You are going to attend an online interview with Business Online. You need to prepare for the interview.

2 Allocate roles. Who will be the candidate? Who will be the interviewer? Think about the following points.

Candidate:
- the skills and abilities you need/have and examples that show you have them
- phrases to talk about your strengths and examples that show you have them
- phrases to talk about your weaknesses and what you are doing to change them
- why you want the job

Interviewer:
- how you will start the interview
- what questions you need to ask
- how you will end the interview

Part 2: Interview

Hold your interviews.

F PEER REVIEW

Think about the interview. Complete the table and discuss it with your partner from the Task.

	Good points	One thing to change
The candidate's understanding of the job they have applied for.		
The interviewer's ability to ask the candidate questions.		
The candidate's description of their skills and experiences.		
The interviewer's job of managing the conversation.		

G SELF-ASSESSMENT

Think about the lesson objectives and the feedback from your colleague. Answer these questions.

1 Did you clearly understand the job description?

2 Did you write a clear e-mail accepting the invitation?

3 Could you ask/answer the questions?

4 Could you ask about/describe skills and abilities?

H PROFESSIONAL DEVELOPMENT AND PERFORMANCE GOALS

Think about the job you would like to do next. Develop an action plan to apply for that job and choose three points to include.

A14

Presentations

Objectives

Speaking

- Can describe skills and abilities using simple language.

- Can give basic advice using simple language.

Listening

Can generally identify the topic of discussion around them when conducted slowly and clearly.

Lesson deliverable

To plan, prepare and give a presentation about key skills for different jobs.

Performance review

To review your own progress and performance against the lesson objectives at the end of the lesson.

Ⓐ SPEAKING 1

What are common differences between speaking in a conversation and speaking in a presentation? Using the list below (1–6), put the advice in the table.

Conversations	Presentations	Both

1 Speak quickly.

2 Organise ideas before speaking.

3 Ask a lot of questions.

4 Nod and smile.

5 Use a lot of pauses.

6 Look at the other person/people.

Ⓑ LISTENING 1

◀))) BSA4.2.20 Listen to the introduction to a presentation given by Phil Haines. What two things does he mention?

1 What is his job?

2 What do you learn about the audience?

3 What is his presentation going to be about?

Ⓒ LISTENING 2

1 ◀))) BSA4.2.21 Listen to the main part of Phil's talk. How many key points does Phil talk about? How does he introduce each point?

2 ◀))) BSA4.2.21 Listen again and complete the phrases Phil uses to give advice.

1 A qualification in Human Resources Management
   ....

2 You .... to have three main skills to be successful in this job.

3 The first is a business skill. .... a good .... to work on your communication skills.

4 Number two, this is a people skill. My .... is don't just to listen to people, but really read them.

5 And finally, this is more of a personal quality, you .... be confident.

6 You .... doing something you think is impossible.

Ⓓ LISTENING 3

1 Look at slides A and B. Which slide is easier to read? Why?

A

You need several skills to be a good doctor. You should be able to remember facts because there are a lot of illnesses. It's a good idea to communicate clearly with different people. And my advice is to be patient. Doctors are always busy, but sometimes people need more time.

B Key skills for a doctor

- Remember facts
- Communicate clearly
- Be patient

2 Use the information below to complete the slide about architecture.

To be a good architect, you should understand science, because that's how you make a building safe. You need to be creative, because people want to buy attractive houses, and they like new designs. Finally, my advice is to learn to sell your ideas effectively. You need to find someone to pay for your building, after all.

Key skills for architecture

- ....
- ....
- ....

---

3 ◀)) BSA4.2.22 Listen carefully to Phil's ending. Make a slide of the key skills for Human Resources.

....

E SPEAKING 2

Work in pairs and practise giving advice about another skill. When you finish give feedback to your partner.

Student A: Turn to page xi.

Student B: Turn to page xiii.

Task

Pre-task: Research

1 **Think alone about the skills and qualities you need for a job you do or would like to do. Make notes.**

2 **In pairs or small groups, discuss the notes you made. Share ideas about more skills and qualities each person in the group would need, or go online to do more research.**

Part 1: Preparation

1 **Work in pairs or small groups. Read the task.**

Context: You work for a large company. You need to give a presentation for a team-building session about the skills you need for your job, to help staff understand the different skills each person brings to a team.

Task: Prepare a 3–4 minute presentation.

2 **Prepare a 3–4 minute presentation. Think about the following things. Complete the gaps using phrases from Exercise C and audioscripts BSA4.2.21– BSA4.2.22.**

Structure:

- **Introducing the presentation:** Who are you? Why are you giving the presentation? What are you going to talk about?
- **Main part of the presentation:** Describe the skills a person should have to do your job. Cover: facts /information you need to know for the job, business skills, people skills, personal qualities.
- **Ending:** What main points do you need to repeat?

Techniques and language:

- Prepare a title slide, and a slide of key points.
- Some organising phrases I will use are: ....^{1}, ...^{2}, ...^{3}.
- Some expressions of advice I will use are: ....^{4}, ...^{5}, ...^{6}, ...^{7}.
- I will invite questions with the phrase: ....^{8}.

Part 2: Presentation

Give your presentations.

Presenters: Use the structure in Part 1. Give your presentation.

Audience: Make notes on the different skills while you listen. Did the presenter give good reasons why each skill is useful?

F PEER REVIEW

Complete the sentences about another presentation. Give feedback.

You covered these things in the main part of your presentation:

....

You used these techniques / this language when presenting:

....

One thing you did very well was ....

One suggestion to improve your presentation is ....

G SELF-ASSESSMENT

Look back at the lesson objectives. Complete the sentences.

I can ....

I can't ....

....

H PROFESSIONAL DEVELOPMENT AND PERFORMANCE GOALS

What advice do you need to give in your job? Do you need to give training? Write three sentences about how you could use the skills in this lesson to help you do this.

1 ....

2 ....

3 ....

Writing file

E-mails

From:	e.lee@bilder.com
To:	tobias.schmidt@schneemans.de
Subject:	Dinner invitation

Dear Mr Schmidt

I would like to invite you to dinner after your visit to our company next week if you have time. Our Managing Director, Alison McDermott, will also come.

I will book a table at an Italian restaurant, Via Venezia, for 8 p.m. on Tuesday evening. The restaurant is next to your hotel in Barchester Road.

I hope you can join us. Please can you let me know this week?

Best wishes
Emily Lee

Emily Lee
Head of PR
Bilder Construction PLC
Box 62
London W1

This formal e-mail is similar to a standard business letter, but usually it is shorter. The e-mail should begin with *Dear …* and finish with *Best wishes* or *Best regards*.

You use this style if you are writing to somebody outside the company or somebody you do not know well.

From:	e.lee@bilder.com
To:	s.carpenter@bilder.com
Subject:	Seminar contact

Hello Sally

I made an interesting contact at the seminar last week. Pablo Almeira is in charge of Research and Development at Rozlin Electronix in Seville. He is very interested in our new training software and wants you to contact him. Here is his e-mail address:

pablo.almeira@rozelex.com

Hope he's useful for you!
CU
Emily

This informal e-mail is for people you know well inside or outside the company. The e-mail often begins with *Hi* or *Hello* and finishes with *Regards* or *CU*. *CU* means *See you*.

Other short forms are:

TX/TNX	= thanks
RUOK	= Are you OK?
FYI	= for your information
BTW	= by the way
ASAP	= as soon as possible

Telephone messages

For a telephone message, write down only the important information. Use note form. Make sure you write the correct telephone number of the caller. Include your name as well.

Telephone message

To: *Danny Randall*   Name of caller: *Brett Sinclair*

Date: *7th April*   Time: *10.15 a.m.*

Message: *Meeting place with Adriana changed from Grappa's to Café Continental. Be there at 9 p.m.*

Action: *Call back if problems on 01699 720 7743*

Signed: *Frank Churchill*

Product launch plans

A plan can be written in list form with bullet points to make it easy to follow.

Use headings to group your ideas together.

Use *will* to say what your plans for the future are.

Product launch – 'Flashy' trainers

Slogan

- The slogan for the product will be '*Your feet will fly*'.

Advertising

- We will have 30-second TV ads in prime-time slots, starting on 25th May.
- There will be large posters on city-centre billboards.
- We will book full-page ads in sports/health magazines.

Endorsement

- We will offer Matt Hawkins, world-class sprinter and holder of the current world record, sponsorship in return for product endorsement.

Special events

- We will hold a champagne launch at the Olympic stadium (with the staff all wearing 'Flashy' trainers).
- There will be a 'Flashy' tour bus to go round schools.
- We will organise a competition linked to the London Marathon, with pairs of 'Flashy' trainers as prizes.

Lists

Make sure your list has a clear title.

Give the points a number and a deadline if possible.

Write your list with short notes, not sentences.

Team-building activities for new project

		By	Done
1	Organise kick-off meeting and dinner in hotel	3/3	✓
2	Weekend skiing trip	15/3	✓
3	Two-day team-building seminar	2–3/4	
4	Move team members to same office away from headquarters	7/4	
5	Every team member should have project team partner	7/4	

Action minutes

The headings should look like this. Make sure you note who was present.

		Subject:	New office equipment
		Date:	19th April 201–
		Participants:	JS, KG, EdeG, CBM, DG

Agenda item	Decision	Reason	Action
1 Change computer supplier	Agreed	Present supplier too expensive	CBM to check companies by 15/5
2 New chairs	Agreed	Staff have back problems	JS to buy by 15/5
3 Take out walls	Not agreed	Difficult to work; too much noise from colleagues	None
4 Install coffee bar on 6th floor	Agreed	Improve communication and atmosphere	DG to check costs by 15/5

Note each item, the decision, the reason and who has to take the next step.

It is a good idea to give a deadline for each action item.

Letters

Start

When you know the name of the reader:
Dear Mr/Mrs/Ms Peng

When you don't know the name of the reader:
Dear Sir/Madam

For a formal letter, it is a good idea to put the topic of the letter as a heading.

Use the pronoun *we* when writing for your company. This is more formal than *I*.

End

When you know the name of the reader:
Yours sincerely

When you don't know the name of the reader:
Yours faithfully

Sign the letter with your first and second names above your typed name and position.

Tilly's Trinkets Ltd

62 Wardour Street • London WC1

Ms Jing Peng
36 Hersham Road
Alton-on-Thames
Surrey
KT1 3JR

3rd May 201–

Dear Ms Peng

Re: Job application

We are pleased to inform you that you have been successful in your application for the position of Secretary to the Managing Director at Tilly's Trinkets.

As agreed in the interview, we would like you to start on 1st October in our Wardour Street office. Your starting salary will be £20,000 per annum. You can take 20 days' annual leave.

Please sign and return a copy of the enclosed contract to confirm acceptance of this offer. We look forward to hearing from you soon.

Yours sincerely

Karen Gilbert

Karen Gilbert
HR Manager

Enc. Contract
Cc: Elaine de Groove
Managing Director

Common abbreviations

Re: *regarding (about)*

Enc.   *documents are enclosed with the letter*

Cc: *copies (the names of the people who receive a copy of the letter)*

Short product descriptions

Short product descriptions are often found in catalogues.

Technical product descriptions are normally written in bullet points.

The text focuses on technical details that are important for the reader.

Product descriptions for cosmetic products focus more on colour, smell or taste, and how you will feel when you use the product.

GVC home movie system

- Digital miniDV camcorder with nylon carrier and 60-minute cassette
- 6.4 cm LCD colour monitor
- 700x digital zoom and digital colour night scope for colour pictures in the dark
- Long-play function and digital picture stabiliser

Bianca toothpaste

Wake up with **Bianca**! Bianca toothpaste is made of a refreshing mixture of peppermint and eucalyptus, leaving your mouth clean, fresh and ready to start the day.

Short company profiles

Short company profiles are often found in publicity material.

They tell the customer what your company does.

They should be short, easy to read and interesting.

Make sure the customer can see why your company is the best for him/her.

Use bullet points to highlight the main points.

Basle Banking Services

Our mission

Basle Banking Services (BBS) is the main provider of solutions in the market for business-to-business financial services. We want to be the number-one partner for your business.

Our services

BBS offers a wide range of services, including sales and investment financing, fund management and insurance.

Benefits for our customers

With our customers, we want to create growth. To do this, we:

- connect industry and technology know-how with the financial markets;
- offer new financial products and solutions, which we develop together with our customers;
- give fast and friendly support.

Activity file

1   Introductions, Starting up, Exercise G, page 7

Student A

Spell the first names, surnames and e-mail addressess of these people for your partner.

1   Our Accounts Manager is Li Hai. That's L-I and then H-A-I. Her e-mail is l.hai2@GHN.cn.

2   Our new Sales Assistant is Ana Torres. That's A-N-A, and then Torres, T-O-double R-E-S. Her e-mail address is a.tor6@BTG.es

3   The Human Resources Manager is Tom Sims. That's T-O-M, and then Sims, S-I-M-S. His e-mail is t.sims@albets.co.uk

Now listen to your partner and write down the first names, surnames and e-mail addresses of three other people.

1 ....   2 ....   3 ....

---

3   Problems, Vocabulary, Exercise B, page 23

Student A

1   **Match the adjectives (1–8) to their opposites (a–h).**

1	long	a)	difficult
2	heavy	b)	quiet
3	early	c)	boring
4	slow	d)	dangerous
5	safe	e)	light
6	noisy	f)	late
7	easy	g)	fast
8	interesting	h)	short

2   **Your partner has the answers to Exercise 1. Ask him/her questions to check your answers.**

What's the opposite of 'long'?

3   **Now answer your partner's questions.**

The opposite of	big	is	small.
	hot		cold.
	narrow		wide.
	high		low.
	soft		hard.
	right		wrong.
	cheap		expensive.
	relaxing		stressful.

---

5   Food and entertainment, Vocabulary, Exercise H, page 45

Student A

You are in a restaurant with a visitor from your overseas office.

- Ask about / offer a starter.
- Recommend the Russian salad or soup.
- Ask about the main course.
- Explain *moussaka* (aubergine, tomato and lamb).
- Order the same.
- Agree to order dessert later.

4   Travel, Vocabulary, Exercise E, page 37

Student A

1   **Ask your partner for the missing information.**

What is Mr Asafiev's flight number?

Visitor

Name: .... Mr Asafiev ....   Flight number: ....

Airport: ....   Terminal: ....

Gate number: ....   Take-off time: ....

Destination: ....   Arrival time: ....

Hotel: ....

2   **Give your partner the information he/she needs.**

Mrs Bendhiba is booked on flight TAY616, from London Heathrow Terminal 4, gate 23. Take-off is at 08:40. She arrives in Berlin at 11:25 . She is staying at the Metropole Hotel.

3   **Check the information with your partner.**

6   Buying and selling, Skills, Exercise C, page 58

Student A

You are the Store Manager of a lighting equipment store. You are at a trade fair and you want to buy some table lamps for your store.

Use these prompts to prepare your questions. Ask the manufacturer about:

- the most popular model (*What / your / most popular model?*)
- the target market (*What / your target market?*)
- the features (*What / special features / have?*)
- its weight and measurements (*How much / weigh? How tall / the lamp?*)
- the colours (*What colours / come in?*)
- the cost (*How much / cost?*)
- the delivery (*When / deliver / the lamp?*)

If you like the product, say how many lamps you want to order.

7   People, Skills, Exercise E, page 72

Student A

Office worker

You work for a car-hire company near an airport. You want to come to work at 9.30 a.m. instead of 9.00 a.m. because:

- you have to take your son to school before you begin work. Your partner goes to work early in the morning.
- your new house is further from the airport. You drive to work, but the traffic is bad.
- you are doing an extra part-time job in the evening. You get to bed very late.

8   Advertising, Starting up, Exercise A, page 74

1 c   2 a   3 b   4 c   5 b   6 a   7 b   8 b   9 b

9   Companies, Starting up, Exercise A, page 82

1 b   2 b (It's Italian.)   3 a   4 b   5 a (over 2 million)

6 a (398,000m² in Everett, Washington)   7 b   8 c (It's based in Redmond, Washington.)

9 b (21.5 million units)   10 c (for the 4th year running in 2011)

1 Introductions, Vocabulary, Exercise C, page 8

Student A

Ask about: Answer Student B's questions about:

1	McDonald's	2	Samsung – Korean
3	Ikea	4	Zara – Spanish
5	Prada	6	Gazprom – Russian
7	Michelin	8	Mercedes – German
9	Telcel	10	Tata Group – Indian
11	Petrobras	12	Tesco – British

3 Problems, Language focus 1, Exercise C, page 25

Student A

1 You start work at 7.30 a.m.

2 You finish work at 4.30 a.m.

3 You work in Frankfurt.

4 You report to the Financial Director.

5 You never work at the weekend.

4 Travel, Skills, Exercise C, page 42

Student A

You are a business traveller. You phone Big Bird Airways to book tickets for yourself and a colleague.

- Give your name. Ask for two premium economy tickets to New York on 4th June, returning on 9th June.
- Ask the price.
- Ask if there is a pick-up service and car hire.
- Give your credit-card details:
  American Express number: 3871 2239 1026 8892
  Expiry date: 08/15   Security number: 445

5 Food and entertaining, Case study, Task, page 51

Student A

Customer: Tiffany (American)

She prefers:
- hot, spicy food
- quiet restaurants, no music
- restaurants in the centre.

She does not like:
- seafood
- travelling a long distance by car.

If there is no spicy food, she sometimes orders a meat dish.

6 Buying and selling, Case study, Task, page 59

Student A

RC1 SPACESHIP TOY

Manufacturer: Toys Unlimited

Product description: a radio-controlled spaceship, made of plastic and steel;
goes backwards and forwards; can turn 360 degrees.

Price: $40

Target market: children aged 3+

Colours: blue and green

Selling points: Press a button and the front rises; hand control easy to use.

Discounts: 5% for new customer, 3% for early payment

8 Advertising, Skills, Exercise D, page 80

Student A

You start the meeting with a suggested name for the biscuits.

Name: Classic Taste

Price: €3

Promotion: Advertise in top-class magazines and quality newspapers

9 Companies, Case study, Task, page 89

Student A

Position:	Advertising Manager, Omnia Supermarkets Head office: Paris, France
Duties:	• plan advertising campaign • prepare budgets • lead and motivate staff
Company profile:	A group of supermarkets and convenience stores in France; sells food, household products and furniture
Employees:	Approximately 1,500
Turnover:	€220 million
Profit:	€18.4 million
Competitors:	Carrefour, Auchamp, other supermarket chains
Plans:	• to build more convenience stores • to sell more 'own label' products

11 Cultures, Language focus 2, Exercise F, page 110

Requests	Replies
You want:	
last month's production figures	Yes – e-mail them this p.m.
a meeting with the Quality Manager	No – away on holiday
a copy of the quality report	No – not ready yet
a hotel near the company	Yes – book a room at …
the agenda for your visit	Yes – send it later today

12 Jobs, Case study, Task, page 119

Student A

Vice-President of Human Resources

It is your task to interview the candidate,
then decide if you wish to hire him/her.

1 Ask questions about the candidate:

- What area of the company he/she is interested in
- What position he/she is applying for
- Why he/she wants a job with your company
- What his/her personal qualities are
- What his/her skills and abilities are
- What qualifications he/she has
- What work experience he/she has
- What his/her interests are

2 Ask any other questions you want to.

3 Ask the candidate if he/she has any questions.

Benefits

You can offer:

- a competitive salary for all positions
- three weeks' annual leave
- a company car (for management positions)
- health insurance

1 Introductions, Skills, Exercise D, page 12

> **Student A**
>
> Fill in the missing information. Add any other information you wish.
> Then develop a conversation with your partner.
>
> Your name: ....
>
> Where you are from: ....
>
> Your position: *Business Manager, JC Electronics.*
>
> Reason for your visit: *to meet important customers of your company*
>
> How your business is doing: *very well – many new customers*
>
> Weather in your country: ....
>
> Where you are staying: *Empire Hotel*
>
> What the hotel is like: *small rooms, but comfortable bed; big television; good service*
>
> Say goodbye.

5 Food and entertaining, Skills, Exercise E, page 49

> **Manager A**
>
> - You suggest a football match and meal in an expensive international restaurant because everyone likes football and international food.
> - You think the Grand Theatre and casino is a bad idea because there is not enough chance to talk. The casino is good for later in the evening,
> - You think the local restaurant and cabaret/dancing show is a bad idea; the cabaret/dancing show is OK, but the local restaurant is too cheap.

9 Companies, Reading, Exercise E, page 86

> **Student A**
>
> Read about Gamesa's progress in Brazil and complete the notes below.
>
> # Gamesa in Brazil
>
>
>
> **Progress in 2010**
> Following a decision to enter the Brazilian market, Gamesa set up a subsidiary in São Paulo in early 2010. Just six months later, in July 2010, it opened its first manufacturing plant in Brazil. The plant is in Camaçari in the north-east of Bahía and employs 100 people. It took six months to build, at a cost of $32 million.
>
> **Current developments**
> Gamesa plans to buy 60% of the components for the wind turbines locally. Currently, the company is developing its network of local suppliers. With strong orders for the coming year, Gamesa is already expanding the Camaçari plant and plans to recruit more workers. It is planning to use Brazil as a base for developing business in the neighbouring countries of Argentina, Chile and Uruguay.
>
> | Notes | Current projects |
> |---|---|
> | **Progress in Brazil** | • developing a network of local suppliers |
> | **Key events** | • |
> | • early 2010 – set up a subsidiary | • |
> | • | • |

2 Work and leisure, Case study, Task, page 21

Student B

Choose one of these roles.

Role card 1

Receptionist

Your job: Receive visitors; answer phone calls; book meeting rooms

Hours: 8 a.m.–5 p.m. Monday to Friday. You sometimes work on Saturdays.

Breaks: One 15-minute break in the morning

Lunch: 1 p.m.–2 p.m. You never go out for lunch because the restaurants in the area are very expensive.

Feelings about job:

You are *not* happy.

- The reception desk is always very busy, so the work is tiring and stressful.
- You have a two-year-old daughter. You take her to a childminder every morning before you go to work. The childminding is very expensive.
- You want more flexible hours, longer breaks, a restaurant and a free day-care centre in the company.

Role card 2

Website developer

Your job: Build software programs; design web pages, graphics and images; advise clients how to improve their software

Hours: 8 a.m.–5 p.m., but often later and at the weekend

Breaks: No regular breaks

Lunch: You usually have a sandwich at your desk.

Feelings about job:

You enjoy the job. You like your colleagues, but you do not like your boss because he:

- does not give you clear goals
- tries to tell you how to do your job
- asks you to give him reports each day about your work.

Role card 3

Writer

Your job: Write creative, original content for company websites; research topics on the Internet

Hours: 9 a.m.–5 p.m., often later

Breaks: No regular breaks

Lunch: Flexible times

Feelings about job:

You are very unhappy because you:

- are always under pressure and stressed. The company needs more content writers.
- want to spend two days a week working at home. The owners won't let you do this.
- want the company to provide free private health care.

Role card 4

Graphic designer

Your job: Meet clients to discuss what they want; produce new ideas for clients and help them to improve their website design

Hours: No fixed times, but always very long hours

Breaks: No fixed times

Lunch: You always have lunch at your desk. Usually fast food / a takeaway meal.

Feelings about job:

You want to leave the company because:

- the owners do not listen to you when the website developers and designers discuss new projects.
- the owners get angry if you have a hospital or dental appointment, or when you are late because you take the children to school.
- some of the younger designers need training, but the owners do not want to send them on training courses.

1 Introductions, Starting up, Exercise G, page 7

Student B

Listen to your partner and write down the first names, surnames and e-mail addresses of three people.

1 .... 2 .... 3 ....

Now spell the first names, surnames and e-mail addresses of these people for your partner.

1 The Production Manager is Olga Karpyn. That's O-L-G-A for Olga, and then Karpyn K-A-R-P-Y-N. Her e-mail is karpyn@VLK.pl

2 Our Marketing Manager is Kaori Monchi. That's K-A-O-R-I, and then Monchi M-O-N-C-H-I. Her e-mail is k.mon23@ILG.jp

3 The new Customer Service Manager is Leila Mehrzad. That's Leila L-E-I-L-A, and Mehrzad M-E-H-R-Z-A-D. Her e-mail is l.mehrzad@petco.sa

---

4 Travel, Skills, Exercise C, page 42

Student B

You are a reservations executive at Big Bird Airways. A customer phones to buy tickets.

- Answer the phone and give the name of the company.

- Check if booking is for business or economy class.

- Ticket prices: economy £550, premium economy £770, business £999

- Pick-up service: no
  Car hire: yes

- Ask for credit-card details.

---

5 Food and entertaining, Skills, Exercise E, page 49

Manager B

- You suggest a local restaurant and cabaret/dancing show because it is good for visitors to try local food and the cabaret/dancing show is exciting to watch.

- You think the football match is a bad idea because some of the visitors are women.
  You think the international restaurant is too expensive.

- You think the casino is a bad idea because not everyone likes to gamble.
  The Grand Theatre is good for early in the evening. The play is interesting.

---

6 Buying and selling, Skills, Exercise C, page 58

Student B

You are a salesperson for a lighting equipment manufacturer. You are at a trade fair and a Store Manager is asking you about one of your lights. Read the description of the light and answer the Store Manager's questions. Add any other details you wish.

- Your most popular model: AC50
- Target market: students, musicians
- Features: bends in all directions, long-lasting batteries and bulbs
- Weight: 4.5kg
- Measurements: 65cm high x 35cm wide
- Colours: black, blue, brown
- Price: 48 euros
- Delivery: within three days

Working across cultures 2, Exercise A, page 60

---

1 Germany   2 the US   3 China

---

3 Problems, Vocabulary, Exercise B, page 23

Student B

1 **Match the adjectives (1–8) to their opposites (a–h).**

1	big	a)	wide	
2	hot	b)	wrong	
3	narrow	c)	hard	
4	high	d)	stressful	
5	soft	e)	cold	
6	right	f)	low	
7	cheap	g)	expensive	
8	relaxing	h)	small	

2 **Now answer your partner's questions.**

The opposite of	long	is	short.
	heavy		light.
	early		late.
	slow		fast.
	safe		dangerous.
	noisy		quiet.
	easy		difficult.
	interesting		boring.

3 **Your partner has the answers to Exercise 1. Ask him/her questions to check your answers.**

What's the opposite of 'big'?

---

4 Travel, Language focus 1, Exercise G, page 39

Student B

Part 1

A visitor from head office (Student A) contacts you about a visit. Use the notes to answer his/her questions.

A: *Can I rent a car at the airport?*

B: *No, you can't. It's a very small airport.*

- No, ... It's too far. You need to take a taxi.
- No, ... It's a very small airport.
- Yes, ... We have Wi-Fi.
- Yes, ..., but the exchange rate is not good.

Part 2

You plan to visit one of your company's overseas offices for a week. Student A works there. Ask him/her for this information.

- use a computer?

  Can I use a computer?

- get lunch in the canteen?
- meet you on Monday at 8 a.m.?
- visit some customers on Tuesday?

---

11 Cultures, Skills, Exercise E, page 110

Student A

Manager 1

- You think Ken is not happy working in your country.
  - He doesn't understand the culture.
  - He isn't interested in learning the country's language or its customs.
  - He's often late for work and for meetings.
  - He doesn't shake hands with other staff at the beginning of the day, but everyone else does.
  - He uses first names with everyone, with senior managers too. No one else does that.
- You think it's best if he moves to a different department or leaves the company.

Try to agree on a solution with Manager 2.

1 Introductions, Vocabulary, Exercise C, page 8

Student B

Ask about: Answer Student A's questions about:

2   Samsung   1   McDonald's – American

4   Zara   3   Ikea – Swedish

6   Gazprom   5   Prada   Italian

8   Mercedes   7   Michelin – French

10 Tata Group   9   Telcel- Mexican

12 Tesco   11 Petrobras – Brazilian

3 Problems, Case study, Task, page 29

Student B

Manager at High-Style Business Rentals

You receive a telephone call from an unhappy guest.

- Listen to the guest.
- Say you are sorry about the problems.
- Offer him/her a bigger apartment (price: $10 more per day).
- Offer him/her a lower internet price ($6 an hour).

Information: You have more furniture for guests in your building.
You will get some new televisions next week.

4 Travel, Vocabulary, Exercise E, page 37

Student B

1   **Give your partner the information he/she needs.**

Mr Asafiev is booked on flight IB231 from New York JFK, Terminal 2, gate 14.
Take-off is at 07:35. He arrives in Madrid at 15:25. He is staying at the Hilton Hotel.

2   **Ask your partner for the missing information.**

What is Mrs Bendhiba's flight number?

Visitor

Name: .... Mrs Bendhiba ....   Flight number: ....

Airport: ....   Terminal: ....

Gate number: ....   Take-off time: ....

Destination: ....   Arrival time: ....

Hotel: ....

3   **Check the information with your partner.**

6 Buying and selling, Case study, Task, page 59

Student B

ROBOT 'MEMEME' TOY

Manufacturer: WCTV Enterprises

Product description: a small battery-operated robot; made of plastic and rubber; wears big rubber boots; talks in a funny voice, always about itself; based on a character in a TV programme.

Price: $30

Target market: children aged 5+

Colours: red and yellow

Selling points: Can sing five songs; goes fast backwards.

Discount: 6% for new customers

4 Travel, Language focus 2, Exercise C, page 41

Student B

Part 1	**Part 2**
Student A has a new job abroad. You live in that country. Use these notes to answer his/her questions.	You have a new job abroad. Student A lives there. Ask him/her about these points.
A: *Is there an international school?*	• good restaurants
B: *Yes. There's a very good American school.*	*Are there any good restaurants?*
• Yes. … some, but … more apartments.	• tennis courts
• Yes. … very good American school.	• swimming pool
• Yes, … and it's very cheap.	• cinemas
• No, but … lots of small shops and a market every day.	

5 Food and entertaining, Case study, Task, page 51

Student B

Customer: Hanna (German)

She prefers:
- vegetarian dishes
- lively restaurants with music
- delicious desserts.

She does not like:
- meat or seafood dishes
- expensive restaurants.

7 People, Skills, Exercise E, page 72

Student B

Manager

You work for a car hire company near the airport. You do not want the office worker to start at 9.30 a.m. because:

- many people come to the company early in the morning to hire a car. It's a very busy time.
- other employees will want to work later if you let this worker start at 9.30 a.m.
- you think the worker is lazy. He/She just doesn't want to get up early in the morning.

8 Advertising, Skills, Exercise D, page 80

Student B

You disagree with Student A's suggestions.

Name: Take-a-break

Price: €1.2

Promotion: Advertise on radio and TV and in cinemas

11 Cultures, Case study, Task, page 111

Kate Maskie

You want to introduce all the new ideas. You think the:

- image of the overseas branch is not good.
- branch will lose customers if it doesn't change.
- staff will enjoy a more relaxed, informal atmosphere.
- staff will be more motivated and will work better as a team.
- branch office will keep more staff if the working hours are flexible.

1 Introductions, Skills, Exercise D, page 12

Student B

Fill in the missing information. Add any other information you wish.
Then develop a conversation with your partner.

Your name: ....

Where you are from: ....,,,,,,,,,,,,,..... ...

Your position: *Marketing Director, Universal Travel*

Reason for your visit: *to visit tourist offices and get information about tourist attractions*

How your business is doing: *not very well at the moment – too many competitors*

Weather in your country: ....

Where you are staying: *Eastern Hotel*

What the hotel is like: *good value for money; big room; large bed, armchair and desk; lots of lights*

Say goodbye.

4 Travel, Case study, page 43

Meeting rooms and seminar rooms

The Conference Centre has three meeting rooms and four seminar rooms.

The meeting rooms

- *Rossini*
  - Seating capacity: 100
  - Video conferencing, large screen (5m x 4m), no direct access to the terrace and garden, technical support at all times

- *Puccini*
  - Seating capacity: 75
  - Video conferencing, projector + screen (4.5m x 4m), direct access to the terrace and garden

- *Verdi*
  - Seating capacity: 50
  - Film projector and screen (4m x 3.5m), six laptops ($20 a day), technical support

5 Food and entertaining, Vocabulary, Exercise H, page 45

Student B

You are in a restaurant with a colleague from your head office.

- Say yes. Ask about a recommendation.
- Choose Russian salad or soup.
- Ask for help. You don't know what *moussaka* is.
- Choose moussaka.
- Suggest ordering dessert and coffee later.

11 Cultures, Case study, Task, page 111

Stuart Adams

You are against all the changes. You think:

- the staff prefer a formal style of management.
- a flexitime system will be difficult to organise.
- hot-desking will not be popular. Staff prefer to have their own desk.
- long meetings are good for team-building and decision-making.
- junior staff will feel uncomfortable with an 'open-door' policy. It is unusual in their culture.

5   Food and entertaining, Case study, Task, page 51

Student C

Customer: Takashi (Japanese)

He prefers:

- high-quality seafood and delicious desserts
- quiet restaurants with relaxed atmosphere
- beautiful restaurants with soft music.

He does not like:

- hot, spicy food
- long trips by car.

---

9   Companies, Reading, Exercise E, page 86

Student B

Read about Gamesa's progress in India and complete the notes below.

Gamesa in India

Progress in 2010

In early 2010, Gamesa decided to enter the Indian market by setting up a subsidiary. Soon after, in February 2010, the company started production at its first manufacturing plant, near the city of Chennai in south-east India. The plant has a workforce of 100. The following month, as part of its strategy for developing the Indian market, it opened a technology centre, also near Chennai.

Current developments

The technology centre employs 45 engineers. Currently they are working with local suppliers to improve quality. The centre is also setting up research projects with universities. Business is growing fast, and Gamesa has large orders in India and also in the neighbouring country of Sri Lanka. As a result, the company is expanding its production capacity and is building new plants in the northern state of Gujarat and in Tamil Nadu in the south of India.

Notes

Progress in India

Key events

- early 2010 – set up a subsidiary
-
-

Current projects

- technology centre working with local suppliers to improve quality
-
-
-

---

11 Cultures, Case study, Task, page 111

Director of Human Resources

You like some of Kate's proposals but not all of them. You think:

- shorter meetings are a good idea.
- a more relaxed, informal style will help the company's image.
- hot-desking will be good because it reduces office costs.

You do not want to introduce any other changes during the next year.

9 Companies, Case study, Task, page 89

Student B

Position:	Production Manager, Miriam Palmer Health Care Head office: Munich, Germany
Duties:	• to manage and control production • to check product quality • to supervise and motivate the factory workers
Company profile:	makes beauty and skin-care products; sells its products in 25 countries
Employees:	2,500
Turnover:	US$85 million
Profit:	US$10.2 million
Competitors:	L'Oréal, Henkel
Plans:	• to set up factories in Africa • to launch a new hair shampoo in the US

11 Cultures, Skills, Exercise E, page 110

Student B

Manager 2

- You think Ken has a problem but you're not sure what it is.
- You like him.
- He is good at his job and helpful to colleagues.
- He often does overtime in the evenings, but he doesn't socialise with colleagues or attend social events organised by the company.
- You want to keep Ken in the company and you are happy for him to stay in your department.

Try to agree on a solution with Manager 1.

12 Jobs, Case study, Task, page 119

Student B

Candidate

It is your task to answer the questions of the Vice-President of Human Resources and to persuade him/her to hire you. There are positions available in all the areas listed, both at head office and overseas. You can join the company as a trainee, junior executive or manager. You may use information from your own life or invent your profile.

Preparing for the interview

Think about:

- the area of the company you wish to work in
- the position you would like to have
- why you want a job with Nelson & Harper
- your personal qualities
- your skills and abilities
- your qualifications
- your work experience
- your interests.

Think also of questions you wish to ask the interviewer, for example, what the salary is, how many weeks' annual leave, etc.

5 Food and entertaining, Case study, Task, page 51

Student D

Customer: Nigel (English)

He prefers:

- vegetarian dishes
- lively restaurants with a lot of customers
- friendly waiters and fast service.

He does not like:

- spicy food or meat dishes
- expensive restaurants that are not value for money.

5 Food and entertaining, Skills, Exercise E, page 49

Manager C

- You suggest the Grand Theatre and a casino because the play at the theatre is very good and the casino is very fashionable.

- You think the local restaurant and cabaret/dancing show is a bad idea because the cabaret/dancing show is too noisy. The local restaurant is fun, but the food is not good quality.

- You think the football match and international restaurant is a bad idea because the international restaurant is not interesting for the visitors. The football match is good for the afternoon, but the weather may be cold and wet.

6 Buying and selling, Case study, Task, page 59

Student C

SKATEBOARD 'INSIDE TRACK'

Manufacturer: Elite Sports Goods

Product description: a two-wheel skateboard; very fast, doesn't make much noise; best-selling skateboard in China and Brazil

Price: $60

Target market: skateboarders aged 15+

Colours: eight bright colours

Selling points: Skateboards have colourful designs by a famous artist; Jeff Rollins, skateboard champion, advertises the product

Discount: 15% for orders over 3,000 items

8 Advertising, Skills, Exercise D, page 80

Student C

You like Student's A's name and you agree with Student B's price, but you disagree with their promotion ideas.

Name: Classic Taste

Price: €1.2

Promotion: Advertise on posters and websites popular with the target market (young professional people)

9 Companies, Case study, Task, page 89

Student C

Position:	Conservation Officer, The Forest Life Trust Headquarters: Vancouver, Canada
Duties:	• to raise money for wildlife projects • to persuade government officials to protect wildlife in their country
Company profile:	A non-profit organisation to protect all wildlife; it has thousands of members and supporters worldwide.
Employees:	10 full-time employees at Head Office; many unpaid workers
Turnover:	US$12.6 million
Profit:	Non-profit organisation
Competitors:	other wildlife organisations
Plans:	• to organise a worldwide campaign to protect large animals • to contact famous people to appear in an advertising campaign for the Trust

11   Cultures, Case study, Task, page 111

Finance Director

You like some of Kate's proposals, but not all of them. You think:

- a flexitime system will be popular with staff.
- staff should dress casually at work.
- an 'open-door' policy is an excellent idea.

You do not want to introduce any other changes during the next year.

12   Jobs, Skills, Exercise E, page 118

Student B

Candidate for the job of Sales Manager, Tokyo office

Use these prompts to answer the Director's questions.

1   Yes / came by taxi

2   like working with people / interested in Japanese culture

3   good with numbers / speak Japanese fluently

4   stay calm at all times / Lot of pressure / previous job / no problem

5   how to deal with customers / work well in a team

6   long hours / lot of unpaid overtime / long journey to work

7   cycling, watching baseball

8   company benefits? / free parking?

3   Problems, Language focus 1, Exercise C, page 25

Student B

1   You start work at 9.30 a.m.

2   You finish work at 7.00 p.m.

3   You work in London.

4   You report to the Customer Care Manager.

5   You work on Saturday mornings.

Working across cultures 1, Exercise B, page 30

1 c   2 a   3 d   4 b   5 c   6 b   7 d   8 b   9 d

Grammar reference

1 *to be*; *a*/*an*; *wh-* questions

to be
Form

+	I'm (= am)	a student.
	He's/She's/It's (= is)	from Poland.
	You're/We're/They're (= are)	at work.
–	I'm not (= am not)	American.
	He/She/It isn't (= is not) *or*	here.
	He's/She's/It's not	Chinese.
	You/We/They aren't (= are not) *or*	lawyers.
	You're/We're/They're not	
?	Am I	late?
	Is he/she/it	at the office?
	Are you/we/they	tired?

Questions with *to be*

- We put the form of the verb to be at the beginning.

  Am I early?   *Is it here?*
  Is he a manager?   *Are you Spanish?*

- We do not use the short form of the verb in answers.

  Are you a consultant?   *Yes, I am.* (NOT ~~Yes, I'm.~~)
  Is she married?   *Yes, she is.* (NOT ~~Yes, she's.~~)
  Are they OK?   *Yes, they are.* (NOT ~~Yes, they're.~~)

a/*an*

1 *a*/*an* with singular nouns

  - We use *a* before words beginning with a consonant sound (for example *c, p, y, j*).
    a city   *a* European   *a* picture   *a* problem   *a* university

  - We use *an* before words beginning with a vowel sound (for example *a, e*).
    an address   *an* answer   *an* hour   *an* interest   *an* office

2 *a*/*an* with jobs

  We use *a*/*an* with jobs.
  *He's **a** designer.*   (NOT ~~He's designer.~~)
  *She's **an** architect.* (NOT ~~She's architect.~~)

3 We don't use *a*/*an* with plural nouns.

wh- questions

What	's	your job?
	are	their names?
Who	's	your boss?
	are	they?
Where	's	my case?
	are	the files?

2 Present simple; adverbs and expressions of frequency

Present simple
Form

+	I/You/We/They **work**.
	He/She/It **works**
–	I/You/We/They **don't work**.
	He/She/It **doesn't work**.
?	**Do** I/you/we/they **work**?
	Does he/she/it **work**?

Uses

We use the present simple:

- to talk about habits and work routines.

  I **get up** early in the morning.
  She **works** from home.
  They **go** to work by train.

- to talk about facts and things that are generally true.

  They **have** offices in Seoul.
  It **rains** a lot in Manchester.
  She **earns** a high salary.

- with verbs that describe permanent states.

  I **like** meeting people.
  She **has** three children.
  I think he **lives** in a flat.
  I **know** his boss very well.

- with adverbs and expressions of frequency.

  She **always wears** blue.
  He **usually/generally takes** work home at the weekend.
  They **often go** home early on Fridays.
  I **sometimes play** tennis with a colleague.
  Do you **ever go** to the theatre?
  I **never go** to the theatre.

Adverbs and expressions of frequency

1 Adverbs of frequency usually go before the main verb, but after the verb *to be*.

   I **sometimes** make phone calls to the USA.
   My boss is **usually** friendly.
   We don't **generally** stay up late.

2 For emphasis, *usually*, *generally*, *often* and *sometimes* can go at the beginning of a sentence.

   Sometimes, I don't like my job.
   Generally, we take clients out to a good restaurant.

3 Expressions of frequency can go at the beginning or the end of a sentence, but not in the middle.

   Once a year, we have a sales conference.
   We have a sales conference **once a year**.
   (NOT ~~We have once a year a sales conference~~.)

   Does he play golf **every Saturday**?
   (NOT ~~Does he every Saturday play golf~~?)

3 | Present simple: negatives and questions; *have*; *some* and *any*

Present simple: negatives and questions
Points to remember

1 In questions, the -*s* is on the auxiliary verb, not the main verb.
   Does he ***drink*** *coffee?* (NOT ~~Does he drinks coffee?~~)

2 We do not use the full verb in a short answer.
   '***Do*** you ***like*** *meeting customers?*' '*Yes, I* ***do.***' (NOT ~~Yes, I like.~~)

3 Spelling rules
   • For *he*, *she* and *it*, we add -*s* with most verbs.
     She ***comes*** *from Brazil.*
     The job ***pays*** *a good salary.*
   • When the verb ends with a consonant + *y*, the ending becomes -*ies*.
     He often ***flies*** *to Amsterdam.*
   • When the verb ends in -*ch*, -*sh*, -*s*, -*ss*, -*x* or -*z*, the ending becomes -*es*.
     He ***finishes*** *every day at six.*
     She ***faxes*** *the invoice to us.*

have
Form

+	I/You/We/They **have**	a German car.
	He/She/It **has**	a CD player.
–	I/You/We/They **haven't** (= **have not**) / **don't** (= **do not**) **have**	the time.
	He/She/It **hasn't** (= **has not**) / **doesn't** (= **does not**) **have**	a good printer.
?	**Do** I/you/we/they **have**	a ticket?
	Does he/she/it **have**	a reference number?

Uses
• We use *have/has* to indicate possession.
  She ***has*** *a fast car.*
• We also use *have/has* to talk about plans.
  I ***have*** *a meeting this Tuesday, but I'm free on Wednesday.*
• In British English, we use *have got* in the same way.
  *He****'s got*** *a job interview next week.*

Some and *any*
• *Some* and *any* are used with plural nouns when the quantity is not specified.
• If the sentence is positive, we use *some*.
  There are ***some*** *deliveries due in today.*
• If the sentence is negative, we use *any*.
  There aren't ***any*** *deliveries due in today.*
• If the sentence is a question, we use *any*.
  Are there ***any*** *deliveries due in today?*

4 *can/can't*; *there is / there are*

can/can't
Form

+	I/You/He/She/It/We/They **can**	go.
−	I/You/He/She/It/We/They **can't** (= **cannot**)	go.
?	**Can** I/you/he/she/it/we/they	go?

Remember: *can* stays the same with *he*, *she* and *it*. (NOT ~~He cans go~~.)

Short answers
*Yes, you **can**.*
*No, I **can't**.*

Uses

- We use *can* to talk about ability.
  *He **can** write computer programs.*
  *She **can** fly a helicopter.*

- We use *can* to ask for permission.
  ***Can** I make a phone call, please?*   *Yes, go ahead.*
  ***Can** we park in this space?*   *Sorry, you can't park here. It's reserved.*

- We use *can* to talk about what is possible.
  ***Can** you come next Thursday?*   *Sorry, I'm afraid I have another appointment.*
  ***Can** we put another desk in here?*   *No, the room's too small.*

- We do not use *to* after *can*.
  (NOT ~~She can to ride a motorbike~~.)

there is / there are
Uses

- We use *there is (not) a* + singular noun to say that something exists or doesn't exist.
  ***There's a** coffee machine on the second floor.*
  ***There isn't a** swimming pool in this hotel.*

- With plural nouns, we use *there are* with *some* in positive statements, and *there are not* with *any* in negative sentences.
  ***There are some** people in the room.*
  ***There aren't any** flights on Sundays.*

- We use *is there / are there* + *a/any* to ask a question.
  ***Is there a** message for me?*
  ***Is there any** baggage?*
  ***Are there any** good nightclubs in the city?*

5 *some/any*; countable and uncountable nouns

some/any
Form

	Plural countable nouns	Uncountable nouns
+	We need **some** machines.	We need **some** equipment.
–	There aren't **any** restaurants.	There isn't **any** food.
?	Would you like **some** carrots?	Would you like **some** spaghetti?
	Do you have **any** coins?	Do you have **any** money?

Uses

- We use *some* to make an offer when we think the answer will be 'yes'.

  *Would you like **some** tea?*   *Yes, I would.*
  *Can I offer you **some** coffee?*   *Yes, please.*

- We use *any* to make an offer when we don't know the answer.

  *Do you want **any** coffee?*   *No, thank you.*

Countable and uncountable nouns

1 Countable nouns include individual things, people and places and have a plural.

   a computer   *some computers*
   a secretary   *two secretaries*
   a restaurant   *good restaurants*

2 We do not use *a/an* with uncountable nouns. They do not have a plural.

   *It's difficult to find **good staff.***   (NOT a good staff)
   *I don't often use **public transport**.*   (NOT public transports)

many, much and *a lot of*

1 We can use *many* or *a lot of* in positive statements.

   *I have **many** English customers.*
   *I've got **a lot of** English customers.*
   Many is more formal than *a lot of*.

2 We do not normally use *much* in positive statements.

   *They've got **a lot of** money.*   (NOT much money)

3 We use *many* with plural countable nouns in questions and negative sentences.

   *Do you have **many** visitors?*
   *There aren't **many** vegetarian restaurants.*

4 We use *much* with uncountable nouns in questions and negative sentences.

   *Do you do **much** advertising?*
   *I don't have **much** time.*

5 We use *a lot of* in positive and negative sentences and questions with both plural countable and uncountable nouns.

   *I have **a lot of** baggage.*   *I have **a lot of** bags.*
   *We don't have **a lot of** time.*   *We don't have **a lot of** books.*
   *Do you have **a lot of** money?*   *Do you have **a lot of** American clients?*

6 Past simple; past time references

Past simple

Form

1 Regular verbs

Verb	Ending	Example
Ends in a consonant (e.g. *work*)	+ *-ed*	I **worked** at home yesterday.
Ends in *-e* (e.g. *decide*)	+ *-d*	He **decided** to take a taxi.
Ends in a consonant + *y* (e.g. *study*)	change *-y* to *-ied*	She **studied** law at university.
Ends with a consonant + vowel + consonant (e.g. *stop*)	double the final consonant + *-ed*	They **stopped** smoking two years ago.

But if the final consonant is in an unstressed syllable, we do not double it (e.g. *develop → developed*; *market → marketed*).

2 Irregular verbs

Many frequently used verbs are irregular.

buy – bought   cost – cost   know – knew   make – made

meet – met   put – put   send – sent   write – wrote

(See the list of irregular verbs, page 157.)

Uses

We use the past simple to talk about a:

- completed single action in the past.

  *He **met** her at the sales conference.*
  *We **gave** them a lot of money.*

- past state that is now finished.

  *I **lived** in Italy in 1999.*
  *We **had** an agent in Asia at that time.*

- repeated action in the past.

  *We **went** to the beach every day.*
  *I always **wrote** to him in English.*

Past time references

1 We use the past simple with expressions that refer to a definite moment or period in the past.

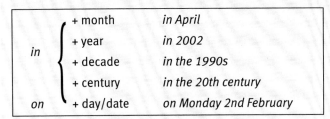

in	+ month	*in April*
	+ year	*in 2002*
	+ decade	*in the 1990s*
	+ century	*in the 20th century*
on	+ day/date	*on Monday 2nd February*

*He first **set up** in business **in 1999**.*
*The **1960s were** relatively prosperous.*
*We **signed** the contract **on 3rd April 2003**.*

2 Other expressions

*We **had** a meeting **last** Friday.*
*I **visited** the factory **yesterday**.*
*He **left** the firm five years **ago**. (= five years between now and the moment he left)*

CD2 TRACK 18 (I = INTERVIEWER, JK = JEREMY KEELEY)

I: Which company would you like to work for, and why?

JK: I don't know the name of the company I want to work for, but the company I want to work for has a big purpose, it wants to change things for people in the world for the better. So a company, perhaps, that will produce green energy, or affordable housing for the poorest people in the world, or ways of feeding people who can't currently be fed.

I: What do the best companies have in common?

JK: I think the one thing they have in common is strong leadership. These are leaders who really want to look after the people that work for the company. They want those people to work at their best. They care about their customers and they understand the customers' needs, and they focus the company's resources on meeting those needs. They also look after the environment and the sustainability of the world around them. And they're ethical and legal.

CD2 TRACK 19 (I = INTERVIEWER, JK = JEREMY KEELEY)

I: Which company will do well in the future?

JK: I don't know which company's going to do well in the future, but Rolls Royce is famous for the quality of its leadership, Apple is famous for its innovation and creativity, and Google invests a lot of time in inventing new products for its customers. Fairtrade is renowned for looking after people in the world, and the UK company Body Shop is renowned for being environmentally friendly. And I think the company that does well in the future will bring those elements together.

CD2 TRACK 20

Good afternoon, everyone. My name's Robert Ford. I'd like to talk about our new marketing strategy. There are three parts to my presentation. Firstly, the background to the strategy. Secondly, how we want to change our current operations. Finally, the details of the costs and the effect of the change on staff. By the end of my presentation, you will understand clearly our future plans. If you don't mind, let's leave questions to the end.

CD2 TRACK 21

Good morning, everyone. My name's Nicky Hunter. I'm a director of a medium-sized coffee chain, Fiestatime.

I'm going to talk about our company and its plans for the future. My presentation is in three sections. Firstly, I'll say a few words about our company. Secondly, I'll describe my duties. And finally, I'll talk about our plans for the future.

Fiestatime's head office is in Chicago, and our flagship store is in New York. We own more than 200 stores across the country. Our outlets sell coffee, coffee drinks and pastries. Most of our coffee beans come from Brazil. We have 3,000 employees, and our turnover is approximately 50 million US dollars. Our profit is about 12.2 million. Our main competitors are Starbucks, Dunkin' Donuts and, of course, McDonald's!

I'm responsible for new business. My job is to help the company grow and to hire and supervise managers for our new outlets. We're expanding fast. Next year, we plan to open at least 10 new stores on the West Coast. We'll start by opening a store in San Francisco and after that, we'll expand …

WORKING ACROSS CULTURES 3

CD2 TRACK 22 (S = SYLVIE, R = RYAN)

S: I heard there were some problems with the sales trip. What happened?

R: I tried to arrange a business meeting with our clients in Toulouse in the first week of August, but most people were on holiday. Also the headquarters are in Paris, so I didn't see a senior manager.

S: When did you make the appointment?

R: Two days in advance. That wasn't a good idea.

S: So how did the meeting go?

R: Well, we had lunch first – quite a long lunch, actually. And the person I met, Pierre Dubois, was very friendly. In fact, he didn't seem to want to talk about business. You know me … I like to get down to business straight away, so as not to waste time.

S: Mmm.

R: Anyway, at the end of the meeting, he asked me a bit about myself. I told him I didn't go to university, but I was proud of being a successful businessman. After that, he was very quiet.

CD2 TRACK 23

speaker 1

My business trip to St Petersburg was a complete disaster. I only arranged two meetings in advance, and one of those was cancelled at short notice. Unfortunately, I went in the first week of May, when there were some public holidays. Anyway, my advice to anyone going to Russia is: make appointments as far in advance as possible; confirm your meetings as soon as you arrive in Russia; and avoid meetings in the first week of May.

CD2 TRACK 24

speaker 2

I had a very successful trip to Kazan. Before the trip, I did a lot of preparation and research. I planned a lot of time for socialising and getting to know people before any business was discussed. I printed out all my documentation in both English and Russian. I gave a detailed presentation on our products and was able to answer all the technical questions they asked me.

CD2 TRACK 25

speaker 3

I think my business trip to Moscow was OK. I spent a lot of time trying to build up relationships; because in Russia, relationships are very important. However, I wasted a lot of time trying to get decisions from junior managers. Next time, I'll go straight to senior managers. One other thing is that Russians sometimes like to think in silence before they answer a question. Next time, I'll allow them enough time to answer.

CD2 TRACK 26

I'm going to begin by telling you about my first business trip to Bogotá, 15 years ago. The client I met was very generous and he invited me to his home for a meal. I didn't want to be rude, so I arrived on time. I brought some gifts for his wife and daughter and wrapped them carefully. They didn't open their presents, so I asked them to. I also asked if they liked the presents. They said they did. When dinner was served, I toasted my new friend and his family. The conversation was about culture, soccer, history and literature and seemed to go well. At the end of the evening, he offered me some coffee. Unfortunately I don't like coffee, so I said no.

UNIT 10 COMMUNICATION

CD2 TRACK 27 (I = INTERVIEWER, RP = ROS POMEROY)

I: Do you use social networking sites?

RP: I use LinkedIn, which is a professional networking site, and I'm connected to just over a hundred people that way. I know some people who are connected to more than five hundred people in that way. I also use a couple of specialist professional networking sites, for knowledge-sharing and for sharing expertise about some very specialist topics.

CD2 TRACK 28 (I = INTERVIEWER, RP = ROS POMEROY)

I: What are the business advantages and disadvantages of social networking?

RP: The main advantage for me, I think, has been being able to keep in touch with many more people in my professional field than I otherwise would be able to. I think also there have been times when I have made contact with people who are interested in the work that I do.

The disadvantage can be that other people make contact with me, who are trying to sell me something that perhaps I'm not interested in.

CD2 TRACK 29 (I = INTERVIEWER, RP = ROS POMEROY)

I: Who is the best communicator you know?

RP: The best communicator I think is my ex-boss from about 15 years ago.

I: And why was he good at communicating?

RP: He always had a real passion for his subject – whatever he was talking about, he was enthusiastic. He made sure that he knew his subject very well, and the one thing that made a big difference, I think, is that when he spoke to an audience, he made that audience feel as if they were very important.

CD2 TRACK 30 (I = INTERVIEWER, RP = ROS POMEROY)

I: Which ways of business communication do you like or not like?

RP: Face-to-face communication is, I think, the best for getting information across and for getting things done in business. I also like e-mail and other forms of electronic communication. They are good for making many more people aware of what is going on.

The thing I dislike the most is the corporate newsletter or company magazine. The corporate magazine is always one way, it's about the message the company wants to get across, and is often not that interesting for an employee.

CD2 TRACK 31 (P = PATRICK, J = JANINE)

P: What are you going to do next year, Janine?

J: I'm going to change my job. That's the big decision. I'm going to look for a part-time job, so I have more time for my family. And I'm going to do a course, too. I'm not sure what to study, but maybe something in computer graphics.

P: Computer graphics? I think that's a good area to get into. And what about a summer holiday – any ideas?

J: I think we're going to stay at home. I need to save money for my course. We may go camping for a week or two … What about you, Patrick? What are your plans?

P: Well, I'm not going to change my job, but I am going to move to a new flat.

J: Move to a new flat?

P: Yes, I'm fed up with all the commuting. Most days it takes me nearly two hours to get to work, so I'm going to move somewhere nearer to work.

J: Sounds like a good idea. Any other plans?

P: Mm. I need to get fitter, so I'm going to do more sport. And I'm going to sell my car and buy a motorbike. I've always wanted a motorbike …

CD2 TRACK 32 (J = JAMIE, C = CHRIS)

CALL 1

C: Hello?

J: Hello. It's Jamie here. We need to meet next week. What's a good day for you?

C: I can make Wednesday. How about 10 o'clock?

J: That's OK for me.

C: Great. See you on Wednesday at 10 o'clock, then.

CD2 TRACK 33 (L = LESLEY, S = SAM)

CALL 2

L: OK, let's meet one day next week. What day is good for you?

S: I can do Monday or Tuesday afternoon.

L: Sorry, I can't make Monday or Tuesday. How about later in the week? Is Friday OK?

S: Yes, I can do Friday morning after 11.

L: Yes, that's fine for me. Friday at 11.30. See you then.

S: OK. Bye.

L: Bye.

CD2 TRACK 34 (L = LESLEY, K = KELLY)

CALL 3

L: Hello, it's Lesley here. Sorry, but I need to change the time of our meeting. I can't make it on Monday now.

K: Oh … How about Tuesday at the same time?

L: Yes, that's fine for me. See you on Tuesday at 10 o'clock.

CD2 TRACK 35 (D = DAN)

CALL 4

D: Hello, this is a message for Jean. I'm very sorry I missed our meeting this afternoon. My flight was delayed. I'll call you again later. By the way, it's Dan here, from Chicago.

CD2 TRACK 36 (D = DIRECTOR, HR = HEAD OF HUMAN RESOURCES)

D: I think there are several ways to do this. We've got eight departments in the company. We could simply reduce each department by 10 workers. And then we can hope the other 20 employees will want to leave for various reasons.

HR: Well, that's certainly one way. Another way, of course, would be the 'last in, first out' system. We ask employees who joined the company recently to leave – for example, everyone who joined us during the last year.

D: Yeah, a lot of companies do that. They think it's fair, but I'm not so sure.

HR: Well, there's a third way. We choose workers who are not essential to the company. We could ask department heads to decide which workers they don't really need any more. It's quite a good way, really. You cut costs, but you don't reduce your profits.

D: So which way do you think we should use? Whatever way we choose, it will be important to help those who are leaving as much as possible.

HR: Hm, I agree. We need to give them a lot of advice and help, so they can move on in their lives. And we need to communicate very clearly to all our staff why we're taking this action.

D: Absolutely.

UNIT 11 CULTURES

CD2 TRACK 37 (J = JOHN)

J: I was in Yemen, in the Middle East, and I was invited to a colleague's house for dinner. There was a long silence during the meal. I felt uncomfortable. I saw a beautiful table and said, 'What a lovely table.' My host laughed and said, 'Oh, then please take it.' I said, 'Oh no, I can't take it.' My host offered it to me three times. It was very embarrassing for us both.

CD2 TRACK 38 (C = CAMERON)

C: My friend Peter joined a French company recently. He made a mistake and used first names rather than family names. The staff were not happy about this. It is always best to be formal at first in France, especially when you start a new job. Peter's last company was an American company. People were more relaxed there, and they always used first names.

CD2 TRACK 39 (S = SUSAN)

S: I was in Osaka in Japan, and we went out for a meal with our Japanese sales staff. There were lots of bottles on the table and, after a while, I poured my own drink. I didn't wait for somebody to pour my drink, and I forgot to pour drinks for the others. The Japanese staff looked a bit embarrassed and started laughing.

CD2 TRACK 40 (I = INTERVIEWER, LC = LIZ CREDÉ)

I: Can you give an example of a cultural mistake in business?

LC: Yes, I think mistakes can come from differences in styles of communication, er, which might be true for some different cultures. I have an example of working with a Dutch colleague, who sent me an e-mail saying, 'I don't like the design – change it', which came across to me as very abrupt and a bit rude, whereas actually he was just meaning to be very clear in what he wanted to happen. And once we had a conversation about that, I was able to change it in the way that he wanted.

CD2 TRACK 41 (JK = JEREMY KEELEY)

JK: I have made a mistake. I was working with people in East Africa, and they had urgent problems to solve. When I was working with them, I rushed the work, I got straight on to the business. And what I learned was that it's rude to start work on the business in East Africa before you have asked each other how you are and what's been going on in your lives. And so when I did the work, I found it hard to get on with it, until I'd given them their space to do it.

CD2 TRACK 42 (RP = ROS POMEROY)

RP: It's easy to make cultural mistakes working internationally. I usually write quite long e-mails. I leave the important part of the message until the end, and that normally comes after perhaps some funny comment. It took me some time to learn that people in other countries find that confusing, they don't understand that I am not being direct. They are confused by the humour, and what I am trying to say then often gets ignored.

CD2 TRACK 43

1 A: Could I have a map of the city, please?
  B: Yes, here you are.

2 A: Could you recommend a good restaurant, please?
  B: Yes, there's a very good Italian restaurant near here. It's in Seymour Street.

3 A: Could you say that again, please?
  B: Yes, Seymour Street. I'll show you where it is on the map.

4 C: Could you copy this document for me, please?
  D: I'm sorry, I can't. The office is closed in the evening, but I can do it for you tomorrow morning.

5 C: Could I have my bill, please?
  D: Yes, I'll just print it for you.

6 C: Could you call me a taxi, please?
  D: No problem. Where do you want to go?

CD2 TRACK 44 (L = LOUISE, T = TOM)

L: So, Tom, things aren't going very well with you and Paul. What exactly is the problem?

T: Well, we don't have a very good relationship – that's it, really. I don't think I can work with him.

L: Why not?

T: Well, it's not just me – I think the whole team feels the same. You see, Paul's not very good at communicating. Or maybe I should say, he communicates in the wrong way. He doesn't like face-to-face meetings, but that's the way we solve most of our problems here. He spends most of his time sending e-mails to all of us. He's very formal, too formal for this country. I suppose it's because of the culture he comes from.

L: What about our customers? Does he get on well with them?

T: Well, how can I put it? They respect him, he's got a lot of knowledge … but they don't really like him. Our customers like to meet us in the evening and get to know us socially. Paul doesn't join in. He's always too 'busy' when a customer invites us for a meal. Maybe that's why the rest of the team doesn't get on well with him. They all enjoy meeting after work and having a good time together. Paul's just not interested in that sort of thing.

L: Mmm, it's a pity. Socialising is important over here. You know, we sent Paul out here to help you, but it isn't working, is it? Your relationship, I mean?

T: No, it isn't. What's the solution, then? What should we do?

L: Well, I think the best thing to do is for me to have a talk with him. I'll give him some good advice.

T: That's a good idea. After that, I think you should talk to the team. Explain what Paul's role is. People don't seem to understand what he's doing here.

CD2 TRACK 45 (KM = KATE MASKIE, SA = STUART ADAMS)

KM: I really want to change things in the branch office, Stuart. I'd like our style to be more relaxed and friendly, just like it is at head office. That's the kind of image to show to our customers. It would get us a lot more business.

SA: Mmm … sorry, Kate, I can't agree with you.

KM: Why not? What's the problem?

SA: You see, the staff at the branch office don't want to change things. They've been with us for years, and they're quite happy with the way things are.

KM: Maybe, but we do need to change our style. We need a more modern image – I feel strongly about that. I want to meet some of the senior staff as soon as possible to explain why we need to change.

SA: Well, good luck!

KM: I can see you're against changing things, Stuart. But perhaps some of the staff will have a different opinion.

SA: Maybe … OK, let's set up a senior staff meeting for next week. You can present your proposals for change. We'll see how people feel about them.

KM: Right, I'll make the arrangements and let you know when the meeting will be.

UNIT 12 JOBS

CD2 TRACK 46 (I = INTERVIEWER, C = CANDIDATE)

I: How many jobs have you had since leaving university?

C: I've worked for six companies.

I: Why have you changed jobs so often?

C: I wanted to get experience of sales in different industries.

I: What have you done that shows leadership?

C: Well, I lead the sales team. I'm also chairperson of a local business association.

I: In what ways has your job changed since you joined the company?

C: I now have more responsibility and I plan the sales strategy for the team.

I: Have you ever worked with a difficult person?

C: Well, the boss in my last company wasn't very easy to work with.

CD2 TRACK 47 (I = INTERVIEWER, LC = LIZ CREDÉ)

I: What would be your ideal job?

LC: I'm very fortunate, because I think my current job is my ideal job, and I know a lot of people wouldn't be able to say that. I lead the management consultancy of 35 consultants, and I enjoy working with all my colleagues. We do very interesting work with a variety of clients, and although we work very long hours, it's very rewarding, and we have a good laugh as well.

I: Tell us about a job you didn't like.

LC: Thankfully, that was one that I had over 20 years ago. And the reason I didn't like it was because I didn't think the company treated people very well. It didn't involve them or get the best out of them, and I also didn't get on well with my manager. Fortunately, I only stayed there a couple of years.

CD2 TRACK 48 (I = INTERVIEWER, LC = LIZ CREDÉ)

I: What are your strengths and weaknesses?

LC: I think my strengths come from my work as a consultant over the last 20 years. I understand how organisations work through looking at their leadership, their culture and their business strategy, and I'm able to bring that understanding to my new, new projects with new clients. I think my main weakness is that I can see a situation from many different sides, and sometimes that makes it hard to make decisions.

CD2 TRACK 49 (I = INTERVIEWER, LC = LIZ CREDÉ)

I: What advice would you give to young people starting work?

LC: I think there are three main things I'd say to them: one would be take the opportunities that you're given and really learn as much as you can from them; the second would be to really listen to those around you and pay attention to what they're saying; and the third would be to build relationships across the organisation, because that's really going to be helpful to getting the work done.

I: What's the best question to ask in a job interview?

LC: When you go for a job interview, I think it's a good idea to ask a question that demonstrates you're really interested in the company, and that perhaps you've done some research into the organisation. I'm particularly interested in culture, so perhaps you could ask a question about the company culture – 'What's it like to work around here?' Or 'What are the pluses and minuses in the job that you're expecting to do?'

CD2 TRACK 50 (I = INTERVIEWER, TM = TIFFANY MARTIN)

I: Why do you want this job?

TM: First of all, I like meeting people and getting people to work together as a team. And then I like travelling and using my languages. I really want to work for this organisation. It has an excellent reputation.

I: Do you have any special skills?

TM: I'm fluent in German and French. I get on well with people. I'm also good at managing people and getting them to achieve results together. I love organising events for clients, and I think I'm very good at that.

I: What did you learn from your last job?

TM: I improved my marketing skills and I learned to work well in a team.

I: And what mistakes have you made?

TM: Well, I'm not really patient with people who don't meet deadlines.

I: What kind of people do you work well with?

TM: As a team leader, I have to work with all kinds of people. But the people I like best are those who work hard and are reliable.

I: What are your interests?

TM: I have lots of different interests. As I said before, I like travelling and discovering new cultures. I also like aerobics and skiing.

I: What about the future? Where do you want to be in 10 years' time?

TM: I want to be working in an international company as its Marketing Manager.

I: Do you have any questions for us?

TM: If I get the job, when would you like me to start?

CD2 TRACK 51 (D = DIRECTOR, VP = VICE-PRESIDENT, HUMAN RESOURCES)

D: Let's talk about the new people we want to employ, Martia. What kind of candidates are we looking for?

VP: Starting with personal qualities, we want people who'll share our values, people who are honest, open and reliable. I also think they should be sociable and friendly. You know, the sort of people you like to work with. It'll be very useful, too, if they have qualities as future leaders. If they can show that, it'll be a big advantage for them.

D: So what about skills and abilities?

VP: Well, I think we should hire people who are good organisers and also good at teamwork. They're very important skills.

D: That's true. It'll be an advantage, too, if candidates can analyse and solve problems. And they'll need to know how to use our main IT systems. What about language skills?

VP: Well, they should know at least one other language.

D: At least one. A lot of them could be working overseas, so they'll certainly need to be able to learn a foreign language. OK, previous experience: I think we agreed earlier that they should have at least three years' commercial or industrial experience. Right?

VP: Yes, that was the minimum. We also agreed there'll be no age limit, but we think most candidates will be in the 25 to 35 age group.

D: Yes, I don't expect them to be older than that. OK, I think that's about it.

VP: Yes, but there is one other thing. We should ask them about their interests. We don't want to hire someone who has no interests outside work.

D: Fine. It should be interesting.

VP: Let's hope so. You never know what a candidate will tell you at an interview!

WORKING ACROSS CULTURES 4

CD2 TRACK 52

In the case of team working, researchers have found that there are some cultural attitudes that are similar for the majority of people from Indonesia, Japan, South Korea, Malaysia, Singapore and China.

These are societies that usually like working in groups. People in these societies are often happier working towards team goals rather than individual targets. They are naturally good team players, and it's not always necessary to spend a lot of time on team-building training sessions. The individual is not as important as the group, and arguments should be avoided.

Team leaders must avoid situations where team members might lose face or lose respect.

CD2 TRACK 53

It's difficult to find common attitudes towards team working in all European countries. It's easier to find similarities in some southern European countries (say Portugal, Italy, Greece and Spain) and then in some northern European countries. Here, I will discuss Denmark, Norway and Sweden first, and then mention Finland at the end.

Southern European teams can often be individuals working on their own and reporting to a strong leader. Team leaders need to give a clear focus and direction for each team member.

Many Scandinavians like working in teams, and this means that Danes, Norwegians and Swedes are good team players. However, a team leader who gives orders all the time to junior members is not likely to succeed. Once team members are given a task, they want the freedom to complete it without too much control. It's also important that information is shared widely across the group. Finland, however, is different, as Finns often prefer to work on their own.

1.1 SMALL TALK

BSA1.1.1 (Jw = Jane Wilson, Sc = Silvio Contini)

JW: Good morning, I'm Jane Wilson, the organiser of this event.

SC: Pleased to meet you, Miss Wilson, My name's Silvio Contini from Teso International.

JW: Nice to meet you, too and welcome to our event. Where are you staying?

SC: At the Marriot Hotel. It's near this conference centre so I can walk here.

JW: Do you like walking?

SC: Yes, I really enjoy walking in my free time - but the weather's not very good today.

JW: I know. It's cold for this time of year. What's the weather like in Italy at the moment?

SC: Oh it's very warm, twenty-five degrees or more.

JW: Lovely. Where do you live in Italy?

SC: I live in Florence with my wife and three children.

JW: A wonderful city! Would you like a tea or coffee? There's some on the table over there. Introduce yourself to some of the other participants before the presentation starts.

SC: Thank you. See you later.

JW: Nice talking to you, Silvio.

BSA1.1.2 (WM = Wesley Moore, JW = Jane Wilson, EF = Emi Fujimori)

WM: Hi there, I'm Wesley Moore. You must be Jane.

JW: Yes, I'm Jane Wilson. Pleased to meet you and welcome to our event.

WM: Good to meet you, too.

JW: And this is Emi Fujimori from Japan.

WM: Hi there, Emi. How are things going?

EF: *(taken aback by the informality of the greeting)* How do you do, Mr Moore.

WM: Oh, er, how do you do Ms Fujimori. What company do you work for?

EF: I work for PKX Energy. I'm their International Manager.

WM: Is that a Japanese company?

EF: No, it's Canadian.

WM: Oh, I didn't know that. Now tell me why your government makes it so difficult for American companies to …

EF: Er…

JW: Oh, Mr Moore, let's not talk about politics now. I'd like you to meet someone else…

BSA1.1.3 (VG = Veronica Gomez, JW = Jane Wilson, HB = Hans Bachmeier)

VG: Excuse me, Jane. Is that Hans Bachmeier over there?

JW: Yes Veronica, it is. Come and meet him. Hans, this is Veronica Gomez.

HB: Good morning, Ms Gomez.

VG: Pleased to meet you, Mr Bachmeier. I've heard a lot about you from Jane.

HB: Oh. Have you? And what do you do, Ms Gomez?

VG: I'm Marketing Manager for WXB Electrics. And you're CEO of Bachmeier Components, aren't you?

HB: That's right.

VG: Is this your first visit to the UK?

HB: Yes, it is. Our business is mainly in South America. Is WXB a global company?

VG: Yes, our head office is in Leeds here in the UK but we've got offices all over the world.

HB: Hm. Do you travel much for your work?

VG: Yes, quite a lot.

HB: What do you like doing in your free time, Ms Gomez?

VG: I really love visiting museums and art galleries and going to classical concerts. What about you?

HB: I love classical music, too. In fact, would you like to come to a concert this evening? I've got an extra ticket and I'm going with some of my colleagues.

VG: I'd love to, thank you. See you later.

1.2 TELEPHONING

BSA1.2.4 (RW = Rob Walker, SM = Sofia Marquez)

RW: Dunedin Language School, good afternoon.

SM: Good afternoon, can I speak to Rob Walker, please?

RW: Speaking. How can I help you?

SM: Hello, this is Sofia Marquez from ELC in Malaga, Spain. It's about our booking with you in September.

RW: Yes, I remember; for your Sales Manager. Let me check on the computer. OK, I've found it. Mr Dupont has a booking for a three-week course in Business English. Are you calling about his accommodation?

SM: Yes. He doesn't want a hotel. He wants to stay with a family.

RW: OK, no problem. Can you give me some information about Mr Dupont?

SM: Of course. What do you want to know?

RW: First, does he have a problem with pets or children in the family?

SM: Sorry, I don't understand. What do you mean by pets?

RW: Animals in the house – like dogs or cats.

SM: Oh, I see. No, he doesn't like pets, but children are OK.

RW: OK, fine. Can he eat all kinds of food?

SM: No, Mr Dupont is vegetarian. He doesn't eat meat or fish. Is that a problem?

RW: No, not at all. Lots of British people are vegetarian. OK. I think maybe the Ross family. They are very nice and they have a beautiful house.

SM: Yes. Can you tell me something about them?

RW: Yes. John Ross is a lawyer. His wife Diane is an architect. They are both good cooks. I think they have one son, but he's at university now. And they don't have animals.

SM: That sounds perfect.

RW: Good. I will check if they are free in September and then I will e-mail you.

SM: Thank you. Oh and one more thing: Mr Dupont loves playing tennis. Are there any tennis courts or clubs near your school?

RW: Sorry, I didn't catch that. Can you repeat it, please?

SM: Are there any clubs where he can play tennis near your school?

RW: I see. Well, I don't know, but I will find out and send you details in the e-mail.

SM: Excellent. Thank you for your help.

RW: You're welcome, goodbye.

SM: Goodbye.

BSA1.2.5 (RW = Rob Walker, SM = Sofia Marquez)

RW: Dunedin Language School, good afternoon.

SM: Good afternoon, can I speak to Rob Walker, please?

RW: Speaking. How can I help you?

SM: Hello, this is Sofia Marquez from ELC in Malaga, Spain. It's about our booking with you in Sept …

RW: Well, I don't know, but I will find out and send you details in the e-mail.

SM: Excellent. Thank you for your help.

RW: You're welcome, goodbye.

SM: Goodbye.

BSA1.2.6 [TRACK REPEATED] (RW = ROB WALKER, SM = SOFIA MARQUEZ)

RW: Yes, I remember; for your Sales Manager. Let me check on the computer. OK, I've found it. Mr Dupont has a booking for a three-week course in Business English. Are you calling about his accommodation?

SM: Yes. He doesn't want a hotel. He wants to stay with a family.

RW: OK, no problem. Can you give me some information about Mr Dupont?

SM: Of course. What do you want to know?

RW: First, does he have a problem with pets or children in the family?

SM: Sorry, I don't understand. What do you mean by pets?

RW: Animals in the house – like dogs or cats.

SM: Oh, I see. No, he doesn't like pets, but children are OK.

RW: OK, fine. Can he eat all kinds of food?

SM: No, Mr Dupont is vegetarian. He doesn't eat meat or fish. Is that a problem?

RW: No, not at all. Lots of British people are vegetarian. OK. I think maybe the Ross family. They are very nice and they have a beautiful house.

SM: Yes. Can you tell me something about them?

RW: Yes. John Ross is a lawyer. His wife Diane is an architect. They are both good cooks. I think they have one son, but he's at university now. And they don't have animals.

SM: That sounds perfect.

RW: Good. I will check if they are free in September and then I will e-mail you.

SM: Thank you. Oh and one more thing: Mr Dupont loves playing tennis. Are there any tennis courts or clubs near your school?

RW: Sorry, I didn't catch that. Can you repeat it, please?

SM: Are there any clubs where he can play tennis near your school?

RW: I see. Well, I don't know, but will…

2.1 MEETINGS

BSA2.1.7 (L = LOUISE, J = JURGEN, E = EMILY)

L: OK, everyone, we need to decide which trade fair to visit this year. It's July already so we don't have much time to decide. I think it would be a good idea to run through a few options. We need a few statistics so that we can compare them. Please do take notes to help you.

: The first fair on the list is the Autumn Fair at the NEC in Birmingham, in the UK. I know we visited this one last year but it is the UK's number one event for gifts. It has over 29,000 visitors…

J: Sorry, Louise, how many visitors did you say?

L: That's 29, two nine, thousand.

J: OK, thank you. That's a lot of visitors.

L: Exactly. From 84 different countries.

J: Hm. And how many exhibitors does it have?

: We want as much choice as possible when we are buying, don't we?

L: Right. Yes. It has over 1,400 exhibitors. We went last year and there were a lot.

E: Sorry, Louise, was that 400 exhibitors?

L: No, one thousand four hundred! Fourteen hundred!

E: Wow! OK.

J: How long does it last?

L: Umm … four days.

E: How much time can we spend there?

L: Two days I think.

E: Can we go to more than one fair this year?

L: Well, … I don't know. Normally we only go to one. We have a small travel budget, so no, I don't think so.

2.2 PRESENTATIONS

BSA2.2.8 (T = TERESA, J = JAMES)

T: Good morning, thank you all for coming today. My name's Teresa Kent, and for anyone who doesn't know me, I'm the Event Coordinator for Darby Tech.

: I'm here today to talk to you about the venue for our annual sales conference. Then I can talk about costs. There'll be time at the end for any questions. So, let's get started. James, over to you.

J: Thank you Teresa. So, our choice for next year's annual sales conference is The Orange County Convention Center in Orlando, Florida, right here in the USA. Let's look at why …

BSA2.2.9 (T = TERESA, J = JAMES)

J: So, our choice for next year's annual sales conference is The Orange County Convention Center in Orlando, Florida, right here in the USA. Let's look at why we chose this place.

To start, it's just fifteen minutes from the busy Orlando airport, which has many cheap flights. This helps to keep the overall costs low for our international sales team.

Now, let's look at facilities. As you can see from these numbers, it's a very big building. There's a large lecture theatre, and there are 74 rooms of different sizes. We can book the smaller rooms for our breakout sessions, such as the regional sales meetings. We'll be in the North Building for all of our sessions, so walking between rooms will be easy.

So, turning to food. I know we had some negative comments about the food last year. I think that's not going to be a problem with this centre. There are three restaurants. They offer a sit-down service for up to 200 guests, so we can make our welcome meal something really special this year.

Finally, of course, the best thing is the entertainment nearby. The centre is located on International Drive, the heart of fun in Florida and near all the best theme parks, like Sea World. It's going to be great. So, note the dates – the 18th to the 25th June next year. Keep those dates clear.

So, Teresa's going to talk now about costs.

T: Thanks Jim that sounds …

BSA2.2.10 (J = JAMES)

1

J: And so … this conference centre is very good – Umm it has lots of rooms and restaurants, and the costs are very low. I think it's the right choice. OK, does anyone have any questions?

2

J: So, to summarise what we saw. I think this conference centre has everything: a great location; easy transport to and from the airport; modern facilities; fantastic restaurants; and overall a low cost. I think you'll agree this will be a very special experience, and make everyone feel like part of the Darby Tech family. Thank you very much for listening. I'll be happy to answer any questions.

BSA2.2.11 (T = TERESA, J = JAMES, S1 = SPEAKER 1, S2 = SPEAKER 2, S3 = SPEAKER 3)

S1: A lot of our sales team are here in the States and like to drive to the conference. What about parking?

T: James, can you answer this?

J: Sure. Parking's no problem. The centre has space for over six thousand cars, and we can reserve parking.

S2: What about restaurants?

J: Do you mean in Orlando?

S2: No, I mean at the centre. Are there any self-service restaurants, too?

J: Yes, there are three restaurants so meals won't be a problem.

S3: You said that the centre is near lots of theme parks. Will the cost of entertainment be included?

T: I can answer that one. We have one free day during the conference and a trip to a theme park is an option for that day, at no extra cost.

3.1 NEGOTIATIONS

BSA3.1.12 (GB = Gayle Bradley, Z = Zhang)

GB: Good morning, Chief Engineer Zhang. It's very good to see you again. How are you?

Z: Good morning, Mrs Bradley. I'm very well, thanks. And you?

GB: We're very happy to do business with you again. As I wrote in my e-mail, in our meeting today we would like to discuss the delivery dates for the electronic chips.

Z: Yes, of course.

GB: So, as I explained, we need the electronic chips on Friday the 10th July. Is that convenient for you?

Z: Erm … perhaps.

GB: I mean, it's really important that the delivery date is no later than Friday the 10th July. Is that possible for you?

Z: Erm … OK, we'll think about it. I need to talk to our director.

GB: Are you saying that you prefer to send the chips a little later?

Z: A little later, yes. That's right.

GB: Right. When do you think you can send us the electronic chips?

Z: Friday the 10th is erm … too early for us. I'm afraid it's a very large order. It's not enough time.

GB: I understand. It was an urgent order. We need the chips for some bank cards.
How about Monday the 13th?

Z: Monday the 30th? Yes, that's good.

GB: I'm sorry but I think you didn't understand me. I said 13th, not 30th.

Z: Oh, I'm sorry. My English is not so good.

GB: Don't worry, your English is better than my Chinese!

GB: We can do a bit later than the 13th. But only one or two days later, is that all right? What about Tuesday the 14th?

Z: Tuesday the 14th? I'm not sure. I need to talk to the warehouse manager.

GB: Chief Engineer Zhang, we need the chips as soon as possible. It will be very helpful if you can tell me the delivery date. Why don't you suggest a date?

Z: Ah, yes. If you send us the specifications today, you can get the shipment on the 15th.

GB: The 15th July. But no later.

Z: I understand.

GB: Fine. We can work with that. So, to confirm, I'll send you the specifications in an e-mail.

Z: And you will have the order on the 15th July.

GB: It's a deal! Thank you.

Z: You're welcome.

BSA3.1.13 (GB = Gayle Bradley, Z = Zhang)

1 **GB:** Is that convenient for you?
2 **GB:** Are you saying that you prefer to send the chips a little later?
3 **GB:** How about Monday the 13th?
4 **GB:** I said 13th, not 30th.
5 **GB:** What about Tuesday the 14th?
6 **GB:** Why don't you suggest a date?
7 **Z:** Friday the 10th is … too early for us.
8 **Z:** I'm not sure. I need to talk to the warehouse manager.
9 **GB:** So, to confirm, I'll send you the specifications in an e-mail.
10 **Z:** If you send us the specifications today, you can get the shipment on the 15th.

3.2 MEETINGS

BSA3.2.14 (H = Hans, L = Lucia, K = Kate)

H: OK, team. Thank you for being on time. As you all know, this year is our fortieth birthday. We'd like to celebrate it with a marketing campaign - to sell a very special edition of a toy or game from the past. I think this is going to be our most exciting year ever!
Er … First of all, I'd like you to think back to when you were around ten years old and decide which of your toys or games you would choose.

L: Ah, how nice it would be to be ten years old again! When I was ten it was the easiest time of my life. There was lots of time for fun and play. Now what was my favourite toy?

K: Wasn't it your Barbie doll? Every girl in Scotland had one when I was a kid.

L: Well, actually, no. I didn't have a Barbie doll. My only doll was handmade by my grandmother. She was the most beautiful doll, but I didn't play with her much. The thing I played with the most was my bicycle! I was always outdoors, cycling with my friends. How about a special anniversary bike? That would be good publicity.

H: In a way, but no good for us since we don't sell bikes!

L: That's true. How about you Hans? Which toy did you like the most?

H: Well, it wasn't a Barbie, that's for sure! When I was a kid, I loved Lego. You could do anything with it. It was one of the most creative toys. I played with it for hours. I know we don't make Lego, but we could choose one of our creative toys, one that kids play with on their own … Er … What about you Kate?

K: Well, my best toy wasn't a Barbie either. It was a game, not a toy. I loved playing board games! I would play with my friends, till very late at night sometimes! I think we should promote a game you can play with your friends.

H: Um. Interesting, a toy and a game. So … which product should we relaunch this year?

L: I think we should look at the sales figures for all the toys we've produced and relaunch an old best-seller.

K: Erm … I'm not sure. Maybe numbers aren't important.

H: Umm, I don't agree, Kate. For the campaign to be a success we want a toy that will sell well today. We don't want a fortieth birthday flop!

L: Well, I think it should be something you can play with your friends.

K: On the other hand, something you can play with alone, like Lego, would be more successful.

H: OK. Let's look at the sales figures first …

K: Yes, OK.

L: Yes, I think that's important.

BSA3.2.15 (K = Kate, H = Hans)

K: I'm not sure.

H: I don't agree, Kate.

K: On the other hand…

4.1 INTERVIEWS

BSA4.1.16 (D = Daniel)

D: Hi, this is a message for Adam Johnson. My name's Daniel Smith and I'm the head of Human Resources at World Travel. Thank you for the application you recently sent. We'd like to invite you to attend an interview on the twenty first of March, at 10 a.m., in our Mill Street office. Your interview will be with the manager of the marketing team, Judith May, and myself, and it should last about forty-five minutes. Please could you bring a copy of your identity documents, as well as a copy of your certificates with you to the interview? Could you please just send an e-mail to confirm if you can come? I look forward to meeting you.

BSA4.1.17 (J = Judith, A = Adam, D = Daniel)

J: Adam? How are you? I'm Judith May, and I think you spoke to my colleague Daniel on the phone?

A: Hi, nice to meet you both.

J: Please take a seat.

A: Uh … Thanks.

D: Actually, before we get started, Adam, did you bring your documents with you?

A: Sure, here you are.

D: That's great. I'll just get those copied.

J: Now, we just have a couple of questions for you. So, tell me about yourself.

A: Well, I have a Master's Degree in Marketing Communications from Bournemouth University. I've worked in the marketing department of an insurance company, Insure Now, for two years, and I enjoyed that, but now I'm keen to move into the tourism industry.

J: And why are you interested in tourism industry?

A: Hm … That's an easy question for me. Tourism is growing at the moment. It employs more people than any other industry, so it's also very important in the world. I think there are going to be a lot of opportunities in tourism.

D: Hmm … that's very true.

BSA4.1.18 (D = Daniel, A = Adam, J = Judith)

D: So, what are your main strengths?

A: Hmm, let me see. Well, I read a lot to stay up-to-date. I find reading helps me with my work. And I've joined a few online professional groups. Sites like Facebook are necessary for marketing, but they change so quickly and I think it's important to know about changes before they happen. That's why the professional groups help. I'm also good at dealing with customers. I made some changes to Insure Now's website two years ago, and they had twenty per cent better customer reviews afterwards.

D: Hmm, that's interesting. And what do you think are your weaknesses?

A: Well, to be honest, I've always preferred to work alone, on my own, but I know that working in teams is very important. I've had training on teamwork. The courses have been very helpful. I decided that, when I get more experience, I want to manage teams, so I know I'll need this in the future.

J: We offer a lot of training here. Just one last question: why do you want to work for us?

A: Well, I like your work. I saw your online marketing when I was researching the industry. It's the kind of thing that I'd like to do.

D: OK, Adam, that's great. We'll take a look at the situation here and call you back next week. It was nice to meet you.

A: Pleased to meet you, too.

BSA4.1.19 (D = Daniel, A = Adam)

D: Hi, Adam?

A: Yes, speaking.

D: Adam, it's Daniel Smith from World Travel. We met last week.

A: Hi, how are you?

D: I'm good, thanks. I'm phoning because I just wanted you to know that we really liked you and we thought that you have the skills we need here in the World Travel marketing team. We'd like to offer you the job.

A: Oh! That's great! Fantastic! Thank you!

D: We just need to go over a few things with you and then discuss when you can start. Does that sound good to you?

A: OK! Well, first …

4.2 PRESENTATIONS

BSA4.2.20 (PH = Phil Haines)

PH: I'm Phil Haines and I'm here to talk to you about the job I do. I'm a Human Resources manager. I've worked in Human Resources for fifteen years. It's my job to find the best employees and help them to do their best work for the business or organisation. I know that a lot of you here today are thinking about working in this field in the future, so I'm going to talk to you about the skills I think you should develop to be great in this field.

BSA4.2.21 (PH = Phil Haines)

PH: Of course, a qualification in Human Resources Management helps, and you need to know a lot of information about employment law, wages and benefits. But what about the skills you need? Well, you need to have three main skills to be successful in this job. We're going to look at each of those now and then I'll answer any questions.

The first skill is a business skill. It's a good idea to work on your communication skills. I mean a really good idea. Even if you're really good at talking with people generally, the communication skills you need for this job are different. Why? Because you need to give presentations and organise training regularly. In interviews, you're going to need to make people feel comfortable. And then there are those conversations no-one wants, when you need to talk about work that's just not good enough, or when two people in the company disagree and your job is to bring them back together. So – Number one – have great communication skills.

Number two – this is a people skill. My advice is don't just listen to people, but really read them. When I say read people, what I mean is, you're going to need to decide if the person in front of you is friendly, hard-working or honest, just by looking and listening carefully. Most people will tell you the things you want to hear. Often, they say things that aren't true because they just want the job, or an easy life. Your job is to find the truth. So - Number two - get good at reading people.

And finally – this is more of a personal quality – you should be confident. The best people in Human Resources are strong people. You could try doing something you think is impossible. You'll soon see that feeling confident comes after doing something difficult, not before. And you can't do this job if you're weak or scared.

BSA4.2.22 (PH = Phil Haines)

PH: So, those are the three most useful skills in my opinion – communicate well, learn to read people, and be confident with people at all levels of management in the company. So, now I'm going to take questions. Yes …?

1.1 Small talk

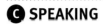 SPEAKING

Student A

Find someone who doesn't like football.

Student C

Find someone who drives to college/work.

Student B

Find someone who lives with his/her family.

Student D

Find someone who likes working long hours.

TASK

Name: ....
(use your own name or choose another name)

Job: Sales Manager
(or you can use your own job title)

Company: Devo Electronics. A global company based in Warsaw, Poland.
(or you can use your own company)

Name: ....
(use your own name or choose another name)

Job: Accountant
(or you can use your own job title)

Company: Bardo Group. An international consulting company based in Caracas, Venezuela.
(or you can use your own company)

Name: ....
(use your own name or choose another name)

Job: Product Manager
(or you can use your own job title)

Company: Vent Furniture. A global company based in Oslo, Norway.
(or you can use your own company)

D

Name: ....
(use your own name or choose another name)

Job: Research Analyst
(or you can use your own job title)

Company: GA Investment Bank. A global company based in New York, USA.
(or you can use your own company)

staff *n.* [U] the people who work for an organisation or business
I go to all staff meetings.

starter *n.* [C] the first part of a meal
Would you like a starter?

in stock *adj.* If a shop has something *in stock*, it has it available for people to buy there.
Are the goods in stock?

strategy *n.* [C] a plan or series of plans for achieving an aim, especially success in business or the best way for an organisation to develop in the future
Our management team discuss business strategy, but they don't discuss employee problems.

strength *n.* [C] something that you are good at
What are your strengths and weaknesses?

stressful *adj.* making you worried and unable to relax
Working in a call centre is often very stressful.

stylish *adj.* attractive and fashionable
Our new women's bags are stylish and fashionable.

successful *adj.* having achieved what you have been trying to do
International fast-food companies need to change their menus to be successful in India.

suit *v.* [T] to be acceptable to you and not cause you any problems
What time suits you?

supply *v.* [T] to provide goods or services to customers, especially regularly and over a long period of time
Green Shoots supplies the gardening industry.

support *v.* [T] to help and encourage someone or something
A positive company culture supports innovation. New ideas and change are welcome.

swap *v.* [T] to exchange something you have for something that someone else has
I use the BlackBerry for business e-mail and to swap SMS messages with colleagues.

target market *n.* [C] the people you are trying to sell to
The target market is young women who want to look good.

taste *n.* [C] Your *taste* in something is what kind of that thing you like.
International fast-food companies know how important it is to adapt their food for Indian tastes.

terminal *n.* [C] a large building that is part of an airport, bus station or port, where people wait to get onto planes, buses or ships
Which terminal does your flight leave from?

tip *n.* [C] an additional amount of money that you give to someone who has done a job for you as a way of thanking them
If the service is good, I always leave a tip.

trade show *n.* [C] an event at which many different companies involved in a particular area of business show and sell their products
He often goes to trade shows.

train *v.* [T] to teach someone the skills that they need to do something difficult
In my last job, I trained staff to use the new IT system.

travel *v.* [I] to go from one place to another, usually in a vehicle
I travel to work by bus.

turnover *n.* [U] the rate at which people leave an organisation and are replaced by others
Nobody stays in the job very long, there's a high staff turnover.

uniform *n.* [C] a set of clothes that people wear so that they all look the same
In many banks, staff can't wear what they like. They have to wear uniforms.

upload *v.* [T] to move information or programs from your computer onto another computer, especially onto a larger central computer
Employees may join chat rooms or forums to post comments or upload images and discuss with other employees around the world.

waste *v.* [T] to use more of something than you need to, or to not use it in a sensible way
We waste a lot of paper, but we don't waste electricity.

work experience *n.* [U] experience of working that is useful in finding a job
Cindy Tan has no work experience.

workforce *n.sing.* all the people who work in a particular country, industry or factory
Dalotek has a workforce of 2,500.

workshop *n.* [C] a meeting at which people try to improve their skills by working together
I run a workshop every Wednesday.

Pearson Education Limited
Edinburgh Gate, Harlow, Essex, CM20 2JE, England
and Associated Companies throughout the world.

www.pearsonelt.com

First Edition first published 2002
Third impression 2024
Third Edition first published 2010
Third Edition Extra first published 2016

Third Edition Extra Premium Digital edition first published 2021

ISBN: 978-1-292-36111-6

Set in Meta OT 9.5/12pt

Printed in Slovakia by Neografia

Acknowledgements
The publishers would like to thank the following authors for writing the Business Skills lessons: Margaret O'Keefe, Clare Walsh, Iwonna Dubicka, Lizzie Wright, Bob Dignan, Sara Helm and Fiona Scott-Barrett.

The authors would like to thank the following for their invaluable help during the project: Santiago García Nuez, Elena Gutierrez, Raquel García, and our students at Giesecke & Devrient Ibérica, Albert Prades and family, Walerian Dubicki and the Dubicki-Pipers.

The authors would also like to thank Bill Mascull for writing the Teacher's Resource Book, John Rogers for writing the Practice File and Lewis Lansford for writing the Test File.

The authors and publishers are very grateful to the following people who agreed to be interviewed for some of the recorded material in this book: Dr Bernd Atenstaedt, David Bowen, Ian Brinkley, Philippa Foster Back, Anneliese Guérin-LeTendre, Angus McCrone, Charles Middleton, Dr Jonathan Reynolds, Marjorie Scardino, Peter Sirman, Mike Southon, Tom Taylor.

Special thanks from the authors to Chris Hartley for his great work on the interviews.

The publishers and authors are very grateful to the following advisers and teachers who commented on versions of this material and contributed to the initial research: Ian Duncan, Andrew Nathan, Nancy Pietragalla Dorfman, Dr Petra Pointner, Michael Thompson, Benjamin White, Aukjen Bosma, David Kadas, Hans Leijenaar, Sabine Prochel, Ulrich Schuh, Robert McLarty.